Chord Workbook
for Guitar

Volume One
SECOND EDITION

by
Bruce Arnold

Muse Eek Publishing Company
New York, New York

ISBN 0-9648632-1-9

Printed in the United States

This publication can be purchased from your local bookstore or by contacting:
Muse Eek Publishing Company
P.O. Box 509
New York, NY 10276, USA
Phone: 212-473-7030
Fax: 212-473-4601
http://www.muse-eek.com
sales@muse-eek.com

Table Of Contents

Acknowledgments

The author would like to thank Michal Shapiro and Klaus Sinfelt for proof reading and helpful suggestions. Doug York for marketing and distribution help. Gary Gold for being the new Mac Guru. My students who, through their questions helped me to see their needs and try to address them as best I can.

About the Author

Bruce Arnold is from Sioux Falls, South Dakota. His educational background started with 3 years of music study at the University of South Dakota; he then attended the Berklee College of Music where he received a Bachelor of Music degree in composition. During that time he also studied privately with Jerry Bergonzi and Charlie Banacos.

Mr. Arnold has taught at some of the most prestigious music schools in America, including the New England Conservatory of Music, Dartmouth College, Berklee College of Music, Princeton University and New York University. He is a performer, composer, jazz clinician and has an extensive private instruction practice.

Currently Mr. Arnold is performing with his own "The Bruce Arnold Trio," and "Eye Contact" with Harvie Swartz, as well as with two experimental bands, "Release the Hounds" a free improv group, and "Spooky Actions" which re-interprets the work of 20th Century classical masters.

His debut CD "Blue Eleven" (MMC 2036J) received great critical acclaim, and his most recent CD "A Few Dozen" was released in January 2000. The Los Angeles Times said of this release "Mr. Arnold deserves credit for his effort to expand the jazz palette."

For more information about Mr. Arnold check his website at http://www.arnoldjazz.com This website contains audio examples of Mr. Arnold's compositions and a workshop section with free downloadable music exercises.

Foreword

To acquire a thorough understanding of the guitar you must build from the basic mechanics of music. Most guitarists begin their study in a garage band playing the songs they like. I was one of these people. There is much to be said about this kind of learning; it develops creativity, a sense of musical interaction, and a soul for music. But although these are unquestionably essential parts of the process, it can only go so far. I found that without proper training I was falling into bad habits and even worse, I felt musically confined and stagnant. Through learning to read the notes on the guitar and understanding music theory I was able to break through this barrier. It added immensely to my abilities on the instrument, and this coupled with my "garage" education gave me the perspective to understand, play, and create just about any music I was interested in.

This book is designed to help you open up to the world of music theory, as I did, so as to know the guitar in a way that will infinitely expand your musical potential. It takes concentration and commitment, but I guarantee that it's worth it.

This book will present you with musical combinations, some of which you may not have heard before, yet these chords and progressions are only a small part of the harmonic palette available on the guitar, and are known by all accomplished players. They are the tools of the trade. Let them inspire your creativity. Learn the chords and progressions in this book and don't just imitate. Use them as a starting point to create your own unique voice.

The guitar is a very easy instrument on which to see fingering patterns. It is a common trap to read these patterns instead of reading musical notation. This can cripple your musical potential. The method presented here tries as much as possible to get you to learn the notes and to understand the basic music theory behind all chord combinations. In this way you can use both your musical intuition and your analytical mind to help you create.

Muse Eek Publishing has created a website with a FAQ forum for all my books. If you have any questions about anything contained in this book feel free to contact me at FAQ@muse-eek.com and I will happy to post an answer to your question. My goal is to educate and help you reach a higher degree of musical ability.

Bruce Arnold
New York, New York

Music theory and chord construction

The first thing a student must tackle is learning how to read music. A detailed description of the development of music notation is beyond the scope of this book and some inconsistencies (which will appear in italics) have stayed in musical notation, in the course of that development. For the beginner these inconsistencies can be confusing but inconsistent as it may be, music notation does have a standard for expressing itself visually and by understanding this system the world of western music is open to you.

Example 2 shows a series of lines and spaces which are employed to create a visual representation of sound. Each line and space corresponds to a pitch. Each pitch is given a name A, B, C, D, E, F, or G. A clef sign is also used to designate what names each line and space will receive. The reason for the many types of clefs will be explained momentarily. First let us look at the treble clef. The treble clef places the note sequence in the order listed below. This complete system of lines and spaces with a clef sign is called a staff.

Example 2

As can be seen in Example 2, each line and space corresponds to a different tone. If you want to have pitches higher or lower than the 5 lines and four spaces you can extend the staff by using ledger lines. Ledger lines give you the ability to represent higher and lower pitches by extending the staff; these extended pitches are called ledger line notes. (See Example 3)

Example 3

If we extend this idea we run into trouble as can be seen in Example 4. When excessive ledger lines are used, reading music becomes very difficult. To alleviate this problem other clefs are employed to make reading these notes that are out of the treble clef's range easier. The note in Example 4 would be found in the bass or F clef on the 2nd space. (See Example 5)

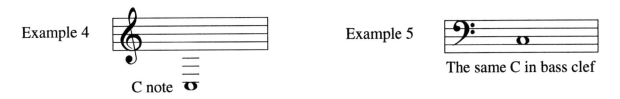

Example 4

C note

Example 5

The same C in bass clef

Example 6 shows where the notes fall in the bass clef. We will only use the treble clef in this book but a basic understanding of the bass clef is important.

Example 6

If we look at our treble clef again (Example 2) we notice that there is an "e" on the first line and a "e" on the 4th space. Our ear recognizes these pitches as being the same pitch but the "e" on the 4th space sounds like a higher version of the low "e". In musical terminology the higher "e" is said to sound an octave higher than the lower "e". If we play these two "e's" on the guitar it would be the 2nd fret on the D string and fifth fret on the B string. (See Example 7)

Example 7

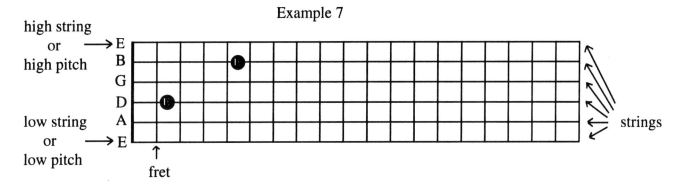

To summarize what we have learned so far: there are 7 pitches which are represented on a staff with the letter names A,B,C,D,E,F,G. These 7 pitches keep repeating themselves in different octaves. To represent these notes in other octaves we need to use ledger lines or other clefs.

One of the inconsistencies of the notation system we have learned so far is that it doesn't show all the available notes in western music. There are a total of 12 pitches used in western music which of course as we have learned can be found in many different octaves. To show all 12 notes in the system, "sharp"(#) and "flat" (b) symbols are used to represent the tones that occur between the letter names of the notes. For example between the note C and D there exists a pitch which can be called either C sharp or D flat. These notes are represented as follows: C# or Db. The (#) and (b) symbols work in the following way, the flat (b) lowers a pitch and a sharp (#) which raises the pitch. If a note is sharped it is said to have been raised a half step; if it is flatted it is said to have been lowered a half step. **A half step is the smallest distance possible in western music.** If we show all 12 notes on the staff within one octave we get what is called the chromatic scale. (See example 8) This scale contains all possible notes in the western system of music. Notice that there is no sharp or flat between E and F and B and C which is just one of those inconsistencies you have to accept with this notational system. Both chromatic scales shown below sound the same on the guitar; the decision to use sharps or flats depends on the musical situation. You will notice that the D in the chromatic scale with flats has a symbol in front of it. This symbol is called a natural sign. It is used to cancel the flat that appears before the previous D. **In written music, measures are used to delineate time, and sharps and flats carry through the whole measure until a new measure starts, unless a natural symbol is used to cancel it.**

Example 8   **Chromatic Scale**

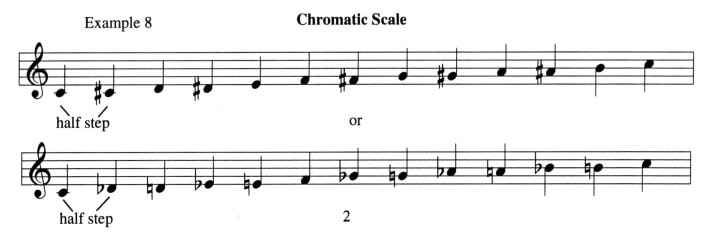

The 12 note chromatic scale can be represented using either method found in Example 8. Remember a C# is the same note as a Db on the guitar. If you play on only one string of the guitar and move consecutively up each fret you will be playing a chromatic scale (See Example 9). If you were to play the chromatic scale found in example 8 on the guitar you would start on the A string 3rd fret and move up each fret until you reach the 15th fret to complete the chromatic scale.

Example 9

Guitar Fretboard

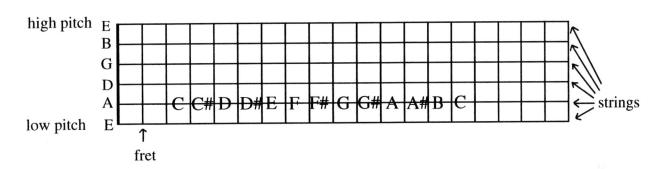

Though the chromatic scale represents all 12 notes, much of western music of the last few centuries has been based around only 7 tones. If we extract these 7 notes as shown in example 10 we end up with a major scale.

Example 10

Major scale derived from Chromatic scale

If we look at the distance in half steps between the notes of a major scale we see a pattern; whole, whole, half, whole, whole, whole, half. **All major scales are based on these intervals** (See Example 11).

Example 11   **C Major Scale**

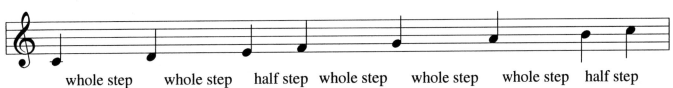

If we apply the major scale to the guitar fretboard the system works out as follows: start on any note on the guitar and move up on one string starting with a whole step (2 frets), whole step, half step (1 fret), whole step, whole step, whole step, half step. This is one way to play a major scale on the guitar. Example 12 shows this system starting on C, which creates a C major scale.

Example 12 **Guitar Fretboard**

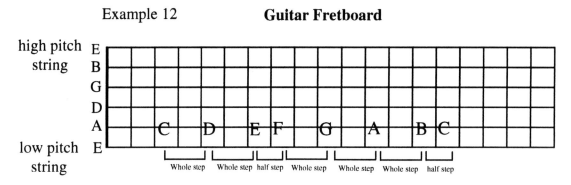

With this information you could play any major scale by following the pattern of whole step, whole step, half step, whole step, whole step, whole step, half step. Example 13 shows a D major scale.

Example 13 **Guitar Fretboard**

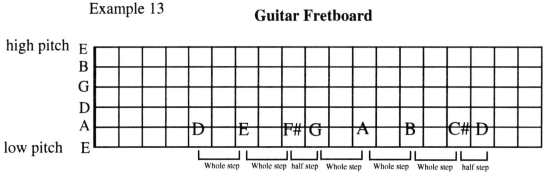

The notes of a C major scale C, D, E, F, G, A, B are commonly referred to as the diatonic notes of the key of C major. If we had the key of D major the diatonic notes would be D, E, F#, G, A, B, C#.

If we use the major scale formula (1,1,1/2,1,1,1,1/2) we can figure out every major scale. We will find that each key has a different number of sharps or flats. If a piece of music uses a particular key, its key signature is placed at the beginning of the piece of music. Example 14 shows a list of all the sharps and flats found in various keys. These are commonly referred to as the key signatures, and they occur after the clef sign and at the beginning of each line of music. The following key signatures are presented using a cycle 5 progression, which will be discussed on page 25.

Example 14

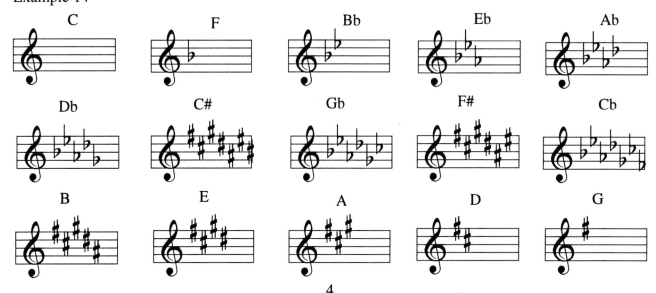

4

Whole steps and half steps are the basic building blocks for the major scale. The whole step equals two half steps. The distance between two notes is called an interval. For example the distance between C and D is a whole step. This is also called a major second interval. It is important to know intervals because chords are frequently named for the intervals in their internal structure. All two note interval combinations from the root of the major scale are listed below in example 15.

Example 15

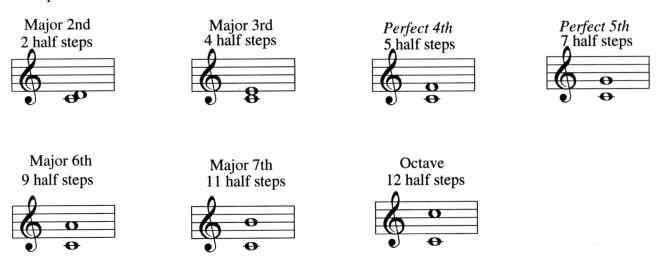

If we sharp any of these intervals we create an augmented interval. If we flat a major second, third, sixth, or seventh, we create a minor interval. If we flat a perfect fourth, a fifth, or an octave, we get a diminished interval, and *if we double flat the major 7th we have a diminished 7th.* Example 16 shows a list of some of the more common augmented, minor and diminished intervals found in the chords used in this book.

Example 16

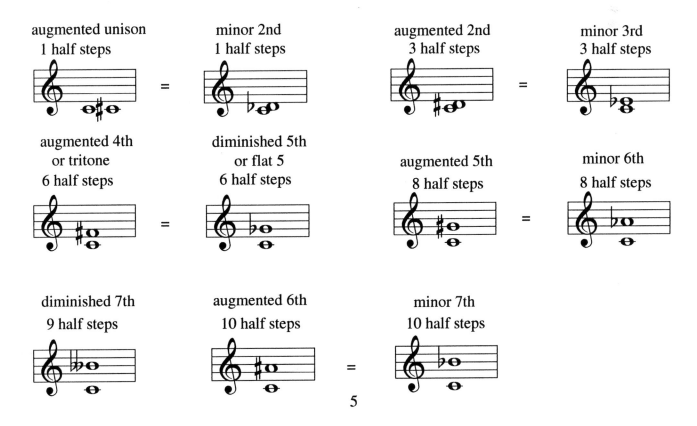

If we continue past the octave, intervals are given new names to show that they are more than an octave apart (See example 17).

Example 17

| 9th | 10th | 11th | 12th | 13th |
| 14 half steps | 16 half steps | 17 half steps | 19 half steps | 21 half steps |

An augmented interval may be written in different ways. A (+) may appear before the number, or a (#) or (aug) (see page 54 for an example). If the interval is flatted it is usually indicated with a flat. Example 18 shows some of the common interval names you will need to know.

Example 18

| b9 | #9th | #11th | b13th | b15th |
| 13 half steps | 15 half steps | 18 half steps | 20 half steps | 23 half steps |

This knowledge of the chromatic scale, major scale and the construction of intervals is a crucial tool to understanding the internal structure of chords. The process of learning all this information will take some time to memorize. Be patient with yourself. Through a combination of rereading these theory pages and studying each new chord you learn this information will become more clear. If is also recommend that you work through Music Theory Workbook for Guitar Volume One to help you ingrain this theory information both in your head and your hands.

So far we have discussed 2 note intervals, sometimes called diads. When we add one more note to our 2 note interval we create a chord. A chord can be a combination of any 3 or more notes played at the same time. Western music can build chords using a wide variety of intervals. One of the most common ways to build chords is to stack up diatonic 3rd intervals. For example if we took C in the key of C and stacked up 3rds we would get C, E, and G because all of those notes are in the key of C and are a 3rd apart (See Example 18). **These structures built in thirds are commonly referred to as triads and the C note is said to be the root of the chord.**

Example 18   **C Major Triad**

If we continue this process and build up diatonic triads above all the notes of C major we get the following 3 note structures (See Example 19)

Example 19

Triads derived from stacking 3rds above a C major scale

These seven chords structures have a certain internal structure. The first structure C, E, and G form what is called a major chord, if we measure the distance or interval between each note using our chromatic scale we can find the formula for building major chords. Between C and E is 4 half steps or a major third. Between E and G is 3 half steps or a minor third (See example 20). Therefore to create a major chord we need to combine a major third on the bottom and a minor third on the top. You will notice that the chord starting on F and on G are also major chords. See pages 17, 18 and 26 for ways to play major chords on the guitar.

C major chord

Example 20

minor 3rd
3 half steps

major 3rd
4 half steps

The second structure D, F, and A form what is called a minor chord. Using the chromatic scale once again we can find the formula for building minor chords. Between D and F is 3 half steps or a minor third. Between F and A is 4 half steps or a major third (See example 21). Therefore to create a minor chord we need to combine a minor third on the bottom and a major third on the top. You will notice that the chord starting on E and on A are also minor chords. See pages 19, 20 and 27 for ways to play minor chords on the guitar.

D minor chord

major 3rd
4 half steps

Example 21

minor 3rd
3 half steps

This leaves us with one last structure, B, D, F which forms what is called a diminished chord. Using the same method we find that the distance between B and D is 3 half steps or a minor third. Between D and F is 3 half steps or a minor third (See example 22). Therefore to create a diminished chord we need to combine a minor third on the bottom and a minor third on the top. The diminished chord as a triad is seldom played on the guitar or used in contemporary music. Diminished is though commonly used as a 7th chord. (See page 9-11 for an explanation of 7th chords and page 38 for common chord forms).

B diminished chord

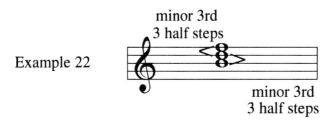

Example 22

Example 23 shows a list of all the triads and their chord names. These chords are referred to as the diatonic triad or chords of a major key. You will see each of these chords labeled in many ways. C major could be shown as: C major, CMaj, C, CM, D minor could be shown as: D minor, Dmin, D-, Dm, B diminished could be shown as: B diminished, B dim, or B°.

They are also numbered sequentially which allows someone to refer to the D minor chord in the key of C, as a "II chord". Because many contemporary tunes are written using only the diatonic chords of a key it is a very common practice among musicians to learn the diatonic chords of every key using numbers and letters to aid in the memorization and quick learning of new songs.

Example 23

Diatonic chords of C Major

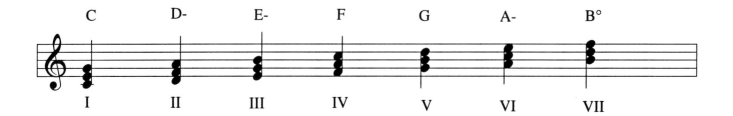

The practice of numbering each of the diatonic chords is very commonly used by musicians to communicate with each other. For example, you might go into a jam session and the piano player might say. "Let's play this new song I've written. It goes 1, 6, 2, 5 in C major." If you know the diatonic chords of the key of C major, you will know that the chords will be C major to A minor to D minor to G Major. So you can see why it would be extremely useful to memorize the diatonic chords of all keys.

If we take the three types of chords learned so far and write them out with C as the root we come up with (Example 24) C, E, G for a C major chord which is a major third stacked below a minor third, (Example 25) C, Eb, G for a C minor chord which has just the opposite interval combination; a minor third stacked below a major third, and (Example 26) C, Eb, Gb for a diminished chord which is two minor third intervals. You may notice that we have not yet discussed the combination of a major third and major third which is shown in (Example 27) C, E, G#. This combination is called an augmented chord and is written as follows: C augmented, C aug, C+. The augmented chord can be found as a diatonic chord in other scales which are not discussed in this book, See page 24 for ways to play an augmented chord on the guitar.

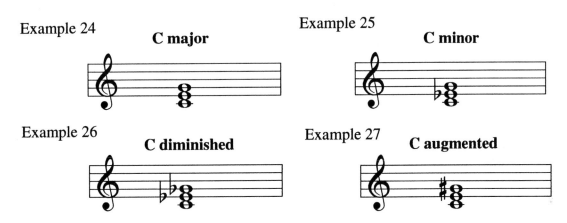

Example 24 — C major
Example 25 — C minor
Example 26 — C diminished
Example 27 — C augmented

There are two more triad chord structures that are commonly found in contemporary music; the suspended 4th chord (sus 4, Example 28) and the add 9th (add 9, Example 29). The sus 4 is a triad in which the 4th has replaced the 3rd. This creates an unusual structure of 5 half steps or a 4th and 2 half steps or a major 2nd. The suspended chord can be a diatonic chord built on the 1st, 2nd, 3rd, 5th, or 6th degrees. It is common to see the suspended chord written as C4, C sus or C sus4. The add 9 replaces the 3rd with the second. The interval structure of this chord would be 2 half steps or a major 2nd and 5 half steps or a perfect 4th. The add 9 chord can be a diatonic chord built on the 1st, 2nd, 4th 5th or 6th degrees of the scale. See page 23 for ways to play a sus4 chord and page 55 for major add 9th chords.

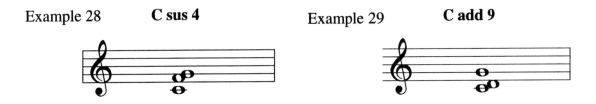

Example 28 — C sus 4
Example 29 — C add 9

The notes of each chord are called the chord tones. For example, the chord tones of a C major chord are C, E, and G. It is also possible to build chords that contain more notes. The next most common chord type is a four note structure which is commonly referred to as a 7th chord (Example 30). To build a 7th chord you add a note a third above the triads we have just discussed. If we add a major third above our C major triad we get C, E, G B.

Example 30

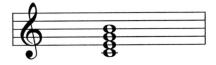

If we go back to our diatonic triads of C major and add a diatonic third above each chord we now have the diatonic 7th chords of the key of C major (See Example 31).

Example 31

7th Chords derived from C major scale

These seven 7th chords structures have a certain internal structure just as our triads did. The first structure (C, E, G and B) contains the triad C, E and G plus another major third up to B. This structure is called a major 7th chord. If we again measure the distance or interval between each note using our chromatic scale we can find the formula for building major 7th chords. Between C and E is 4 half steps or a major third, between E and G is 3 half steps or a minor third, G to B is 4 half steps or a major third (See example 32). **Therefore to create a major 7th chord we need to combine a major third on the bottom and a minor third in the middle and a major third on the top.** You will notice that the chord starting on F is also a major 7th chord. See page 29 for ways to play a Major 7th chord on the guitar.

C major 7th chord

Example 32

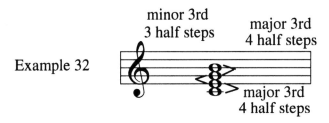

The second structure (D, F, A and C), forms what is called a minor 7th chord. Using the chromatic scale once again, we can find the formula for building minor 7th chords. Between D and F is 3 half steps or a minor third. Between F and A is 4 half steps or a major third; between A and C is 3 half steps or a minor third (See Example 33). **Therefore to create a minor 7th chord we need to combine a minor third on the bottom and a major third in the middle and a minor third on the top.** You will notice that the chord starting on E and on A are also minor 7th chords. The exercise on page 25 covers minor 7th chords. See page 30-1 for ways to play a minor 7th chord on the guitar.

D minor 7th chord

Example 33

The third new structure (G, B, D and F), forms a dominant 7th chord. Using the chromatic scale we can find the formula for building dominant 7th chords. Between G and B is 4 half steps or a major third, between B and D is 3 half steps or a minor third, between D and F is 3 half steps or a minor third (See Example 34). **Therefore to create a dominant 7th chord we need to combine a major third on the bottom and a minor third in the middle and a minor third on the top.** Only one dominant seventh chord can appear naturally within any major key. See pages 21-2 and 32 for ways to play a dominant 7th chord on the guitar.

G dominant 7th chord

Example 34

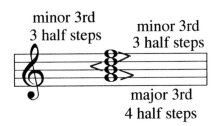

The last structure (B, D, F and A) forms what is called a minor 7 flat 5, also referred to as the "half diminished" chord. Using the chromatic scale we can find the formula for building minor 7 flat 5 chords. Between B and D is 3 half steps or a minor third, between D and F is 3 half steps or a minor third and between F and A is 4 half steps or a major third (See example 35). **Therefore to create a minor 7b5 chord we need to combine a minor third on the bottom and a minor third in the middle and a major third on the top.** The minor 7b5, like the dominant 7th, happens only once in diatonic 7th chords of a major key. See page 36 for ways to play a -7b5 chord on the guitar.

B minor 7 flat 5 chord

Example 35

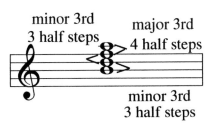

The 7th chords can be organized in the same manner as our triads were. Below is a list of the diatonic 7th chords of a major key. These chords again can be labeled in many ways: C major 7 could be shown as C major 7, CMaj7, CΔ7, CM7. D minor 7 could be shown as D minor 7, Dmin 7, D-7, Dm7. G dominant 7th could be shown as G dominant, G dom7, or G7. B minor 7th flat 5 can be shown as B minor 7b5, Bmin7b5, and B-7b5.

The same numbering system applies for the 7th chords as for the triads.

Example 36 show the chords listed sequentially with their chord names and degrees.

Example 36   **Diatonic 7th chords of C Major**

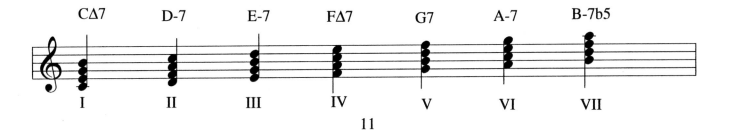

11

Most styles of music generally use triads or 7th chords with or without tensions. For instance, folk music gravitates toward triads while jazz tends to use more 7th chords and even more complicated structures.

If we extend the idea of adding more notes to chords by extending up another 3rd above our 7th tone we create 9th chords. Therefore CΔ7 (C, E, G, B) becomes CΔ79 (C, E, G, B, D), the interval formula would be maj3, min3, maj3, min3 (See Example 37). The 9th is a tension, not a chord tone. A tension in contemporary music is a non chord tone which adds color to our basic triads and 7th chords. See pages 48-101 for all the common guitar chords that have added tensions. Pages 48, 56, 64, 84, 92, 94, 96 and 100 give a list of what tensions are available for each chord type. Memorize this available tensions for each chord type in every key. This will help you add color to your chord voicings when you feel you need it.

The method of using intervals by calculating half steps gets very time consuming as the chord structures get larger and larger. **There is a faster way to calculate which notes are contained in any chord but this requires that you first memorize the major scale.** If we go back and look at our C major scale we can see that to find for example, a major 7 chord which is C, E, G, and B we need only to think the 1, 3, 5, 7 degrees of the C major scale. To add on a tension like the 9th we simply add the 2nd degree of the C major scale which is a D. When the 2nd is placed above the 7th it is called the 9th. We need only to add the 2nd degree of C (which we have learned is the same note as the 9th).

Δ9th chord

 Example 37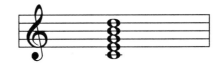

If we use the major scale as our reference point in figuring out chord tones we only need to know the formula for each chord type. For example: a C-7 chord would be C, Eb, G, Bb which would be 1, b3, 5 and b7 in the key of C. Therefore by memorizing the structure of each chord and altering the notes from the major scale we can quickly find the correct notes for any chord. Example 38 shows a list of the triads and seventh chords found in this book and their relationship to a C major scale.

Example 38

triad chords (exercises found on page 18 to 22)

major	(1 3 5)
minor	(1 b3 5)
diminished	(1 b3 b5)
augmented	(1 3 #5)
sus4	(1,4,5)

7th chords (exercises found on page 24 to 36)

Δ7	(1 3 5 7)
-7	(1 b3 5 b7)
7	(1 3 5 b7)
-7b5	(1 b3 b5 b7)
°7	(1 b3 b5 bb7)
-Δ7	(1 b3 5 7)
7sus4	(1 4 5 b7)
Δ7#5	(1 3 #5 7)
7#5	(1 3 #5 b7)
Δ7#11	(1 3 #4 7)
7#11	(1 3 #4 b7)
6	(1 3 5 6)
-6	(1 b3 5 6)

When we add even more tensions to our triads or seventh chords we simply have to add the appropriate note from our reference major scale. For example: Cdom9 would be C, E, G, Bb, D or 1, 3, 5, b7, and 9th degrees of a C major scale (See Example 39). As mentioned earlier see pages 48-101 for all the common guitar chords that have added tensions. Pages 48, 56, 64, 84, 92, 94, 96 and 100 give a list of what tensions are available for each chord type. Memorize this available tensions for each chord type in every key. This will help you add color to your chord voicings when you feel you need it.

Example 39

C reference scale

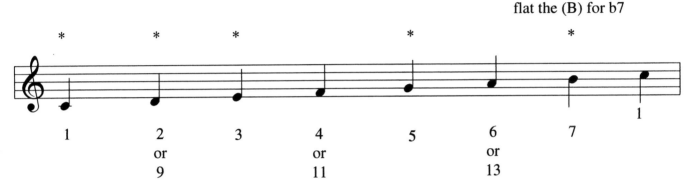

As each chord is introduced in this book the chord tones and tensions will be shown in staff notation along with a list of the notes contained in the chord. Remember that memorizing the notes contained in each chord presented along with knowing what notes you are playing will open up a whole new world on the guitar. Example 40 shows how each chord type will appear.

Example 40

Possible chord tones for C9
1,3,5,b7,9

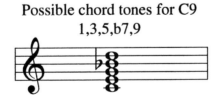

13

The guitar only has 6 possible notes it can play at once so sometimes certain notes are left out of a chord to make it playable. At other times notes will be doubled to make a fuller sound. You will also notice in many places that certain chord tones have been omitted to make the chord easier to play.

Each chord will be presented in its staff form (Example 42) and using chord diagrams (Example 43). As mentioned earlier sometimes notes are doubled or left out in certain chords. Example 41 shows a basic C major 7th chord. Example 42 shows this same chord but with a different "voicing." We now have the root, 5th, 7th, 3rd, and the 5th again. **The combination of notes used to form a chord is call a "chord voicing."**

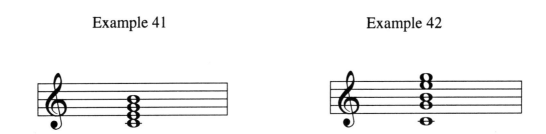

Example 41   Example 42

Example 43 shows how each chord voicing will be shown in this book. The chord voicing is shown in tablature by indicating fret location with the circled number, the fingering with numbers next to the dots and X's placed above to indicate which string are not played. Sometimes open circles will indicate that open strings are to be played (see page 17 for an example). Index finger is 1, middle finger is 2, ring finger 3, little finger is 4 and on a rare occasion T is used to indicate the thumb (see page 55 for an example).

Example 43

position using chord diagrams

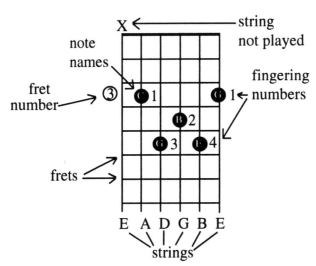

14

It must be mentioned that the guitar is a transposing instrument sounding an octave (12 half steps) lower than written. Therefore middle C on a piano appears as the C one ledger line below the staff (Example 44) while the actual sound of middle C on the guitar is 1st fret on the B string (See Example 45). So if you see a middle C written for guitar (See Example 46) you will play it on the 3rd fret of the A string (See Example 47). All staff notation in this book is transposed.

Example 44

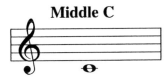

Example 45

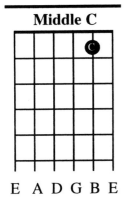

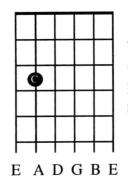

When you see middle C on the staff you play this note on the guitar.

Example 48 shows how the open strings on the guitar would be written.

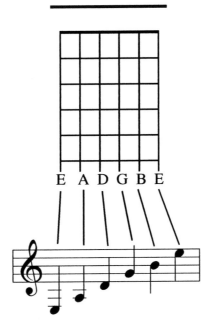

Example 48

Information for a Beginning Guitarist

If by chance you are a total beginner and haven't yet learned the chords found in this book, I recommend you first spend a few days forming and playing each chord. Remember it will take a few weeks if not a month before your fingers develop calluses so you may experience a little pain. This pain can be minimized by pressing on the string only hard enough to make the note sound. Most students that are beginners tend to press on the notes a lot harder than they need to, and therefore experience pain or fatigue after playing only for a short while. I recommend if you are a total beginner to play in five or ten minute intervals with 20 minute rest periods. This will help your hand to acclimate to the guitar. It will also help you to know when you have practiced enough because during your 20 minute rest intervals you will feel how fatigued your hand really is. Because guitar technique is so important to proper development I suggest you buy the E-book "Guitar Technique: Volume One," ISBN 1-890944-91-2. This book contains pictures and links to video clips to help you with the proper technique on the guitar. This can greatly accelerate your progress.

There are two types of chords found in this book; "open" and "barre." "Open" refers to the fact that you are playing some open strings when you play each chord. "Barre" refers to the fact that you lay your first finger across multiple strings in order to create chords that can be moved around to different areas of the guitar neck enabling you to play the same chord at different pitches.

These two types of chords are the ones most used when the guitar is played as a solo accompaniment, especially in folk, rock and jazz. There are of course many other ways to play chords on the guitar. Depending on the style and function of the guitar within a group, different chord voicings are called upon to fill these situations. For example when a guitar is playing with a funk band you would use a completely different set of chords than the chords found in this book. The chords found in Chord Workbook for Guitar Volume Two (ISBN 0-9648632-3-5 or 1-890944-51-3) would be the chords most commonly used in the aforementioned situations.

As mentioned in the music theory section certain chord voicings presented in this book do not contain all the chord tones. It is common to leave out certain chord tones to make a chord easier to play or to give it a unique sound. The chord tone that is most commonly left out of a chord is the 5th. (See page 21: the top C dominant chord doesn't contain the 5th, or page 22: the F7 chord contains no 5th.)

There are many ways you could work through this book. You could just start with each chord and learn a few each week. For some students this works fine, while others need to apply each chord they learn to music, so it makes sense to them. For those who prefer the former approach, the "Cycle 5" progression method found on page 25 is extremely helpful for memorizing "barre" chords. For students who prefer the latter approach there are chord progressions in the back of the book that give examples for the chords found on pages 29-101. If you are a beginner and need work on the "open" chords on pages 17-24 or the "barre" chords on pages 26, 27 and 32, Muse-eek Publishing Company has a "member's section" of their website containing chord progressions to help you develop your ability. You will also find links to audio files which will demonstrate the sound of each chord progression. I highly recommend you take advantage of these help files.

Root Position Major Chords

Possible chord tones for major
1,3,5

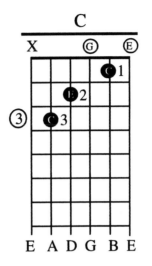

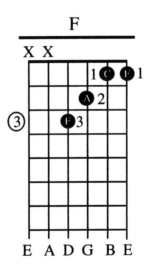

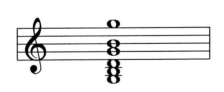
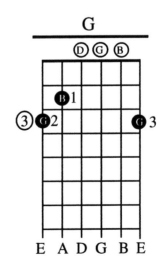

Root Position Major Chords

Possible chord tones for major
1,3,5

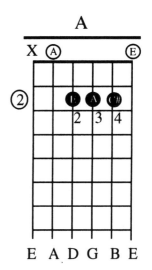

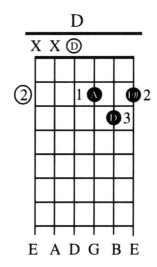

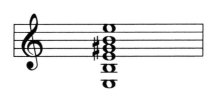

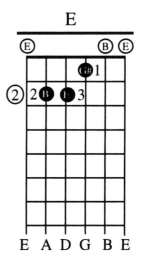

Root Position Minor Chords

Possible chord tones for minor
1,b3,5

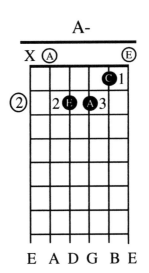

A-

E A D G B E

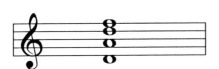

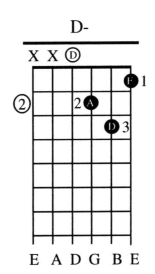

D-

E A D G B E

Root Position Minor Chords
Possible chord tones for minor
1,b3,5

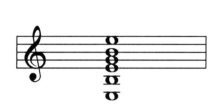

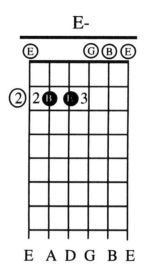

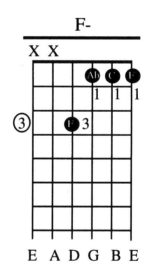

20

Root Position Dominant 7th Chords
Possible chord tones for 7
1,3,5,b7

C7

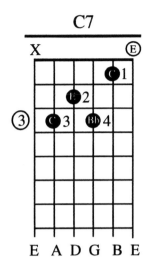

D7

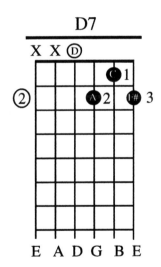

E7

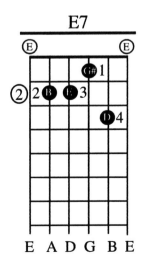

Root Position Dominant 7th Chords
Possible chord tones for 7
1,3,5,b7

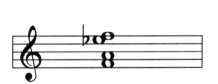

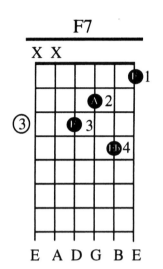

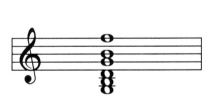

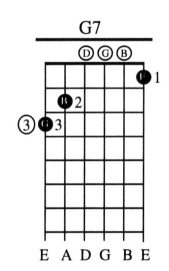

Root Position Suspended 4th Chords
Possible chord tones for sus4
1,4,5

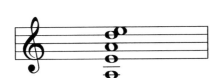

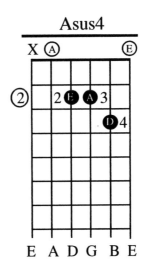

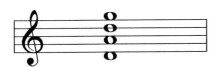

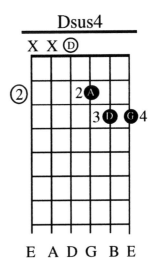

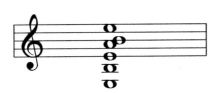

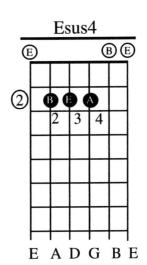

Root Position Augmented 5 Chords

Possible chord tones for augmented
1,3,#5

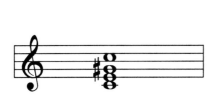

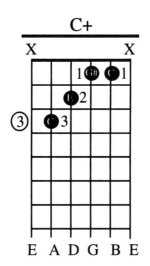

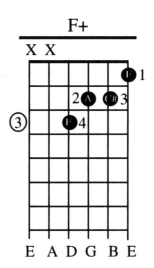

Moveable Chord Forms

The chords that follow allow you to learn a chord form and then move it around the neck to get that chord type for every degree of a chromatic scale. All the notated examples of chords should be practiced "cycle 5". Cycle 5 is a way to play all 12 chromatic notes by moving in a pattern of 5ths (or 7 half steps) down from the previous chord. Therefore C moves to F then Bb, Eb, Ab, Db, Gb, B, E, A, D, G. On the guitar this means you would play for example the first C major chord at the 3rd fret as indicated and then play the same fingering at the 8th fret on the 5th string and you get F major, then the 1st fret for Bb major, 6 fret for Eb major etc. The example below shows you how to proceed.

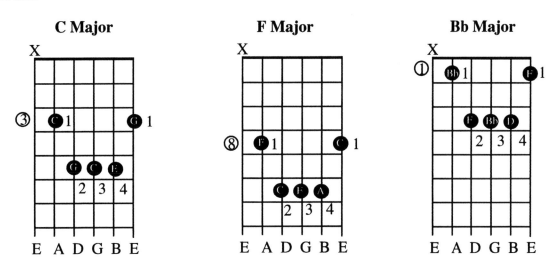

Don't just memorize the position of each of these chords without thinking of what chord you are playing. Memorize, for now, the shape so you can recognize the chord type then memorize the bottom of each chord to tell you which chord you are playing as you move through the cycle 5 progression. Remember all examples in this book have the root as the lowest note of each chord voicing so by memorizing the bottom note as you move cycle 5 you will be memorizing the notes on the E and A strings. When you have memorized the notes on the E and A strings you only need to memorize the new chord type as you move through this book.

Cycle 5 is one of the most common chord movements in music. Therefore practicing chords cycle 5 is excellent preparation for playing music

Cycle 5 Progression or the Circle of Fifths

C, F, Bb, Eb, Ab, Db, Gb, B, E, A, D, G

It is also a good idea to go through the cycle in a couple of ways. For example when you get to Gb think F# instead. Gb and F# are said to be enharmonic keys because their pitches are the same on the guitar but there names are different. Refer back to your list of keys to find other enharmonic keys to practice.

Try not to think down a certain number of frets to find the next chord. Memorizing the pitches of each fret will be much better in the long run. All chords contained in this book should be practiced using the cycle 5 movement, and remember when practicing always think what note you are playing rather than memorizing the position.

Root Position Major Chords

Possible chord tones for C major

1,3,5

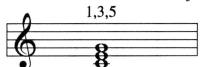

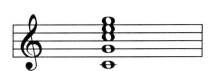

C Major

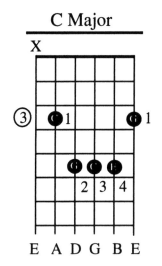

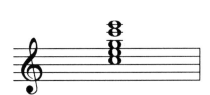

C Major

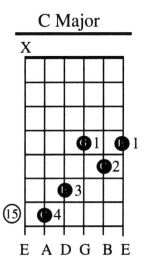

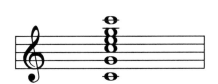

C Major

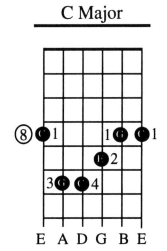

Root Position Minor Chords

Possible chord tones for C-
1,b3,5

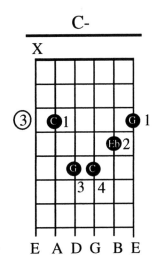

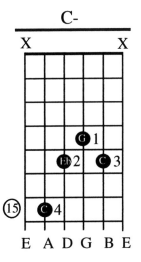

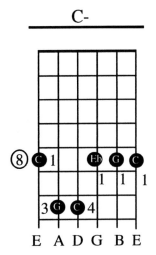

Root Position Augmented 5th Chords

Possible chord tones for C augmented
1,3,#5

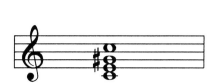

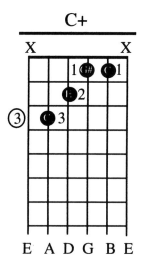

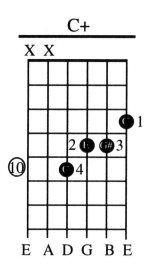

Root Position Major 7th Chords

Possible chord tones for CΔ7

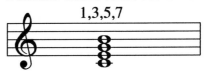

1,3,5,7

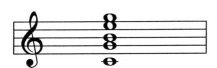

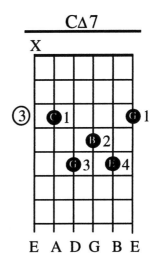

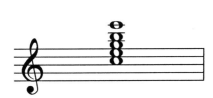

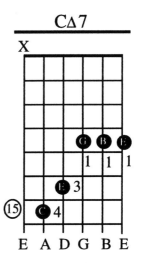

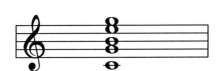

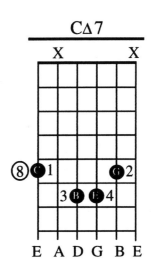

29

Root Position Minor 7th Chords

Possible chord tones for C-7

1,b3,5,b7

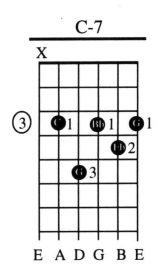

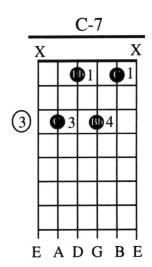

Root Position Minor 7th Chords

Possible chord tones for C-7
1,b3,5,b7

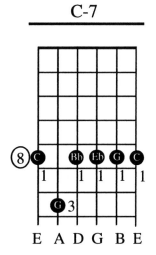

C-7

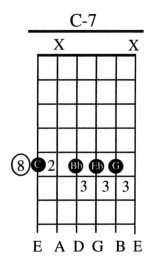

C-7

Root Position Dominant 7th Chords

Possible chord tones for C7
1,3,5,b7

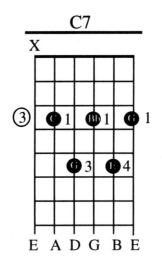

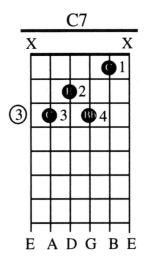

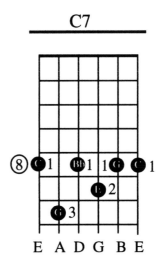

Chord progressions for practice

Below are listed a few chord progression to gain familarity with the moveable chords forms learned so far. A very common progression is II-V-I. In C that would be D-7 G7 CΔ7 and is shown below. This II-V-I progression should be practiced cycle 5.

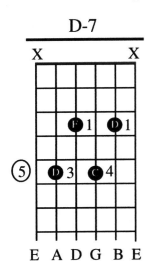
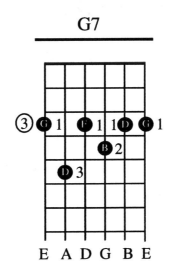
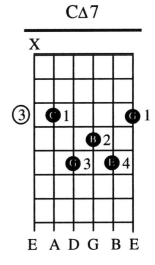

To practice this progression cycle 5 you would proceed as follows:

1. D-7 G7 CΔ7   7. Ab-7 Db7 GbΔ7
2. G-7 C7 FΔ7   8. C#-7 F#7 BΔ7
3. C-7 F7 BbΔ7   9. F#-7 B7 EΔ7
4. F-7 Bb7 EbΔ7   10. B-7 E7 AΔ7
5. Bb-7 Eb7 AbΔ7   11. E-7 A7 DΔ7
6. Eb-7 Ab7 DbΔ7   12. A-7 D7 GΔ7

Another possible way of playing this II-V-I progression is listed below. There are many more ways of combining the II -7, V dom7, to I Δ7 using all the chord voicings you have learned so far. Make sure you know all the possibilities.

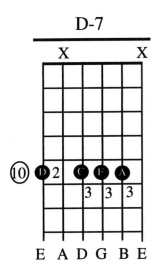
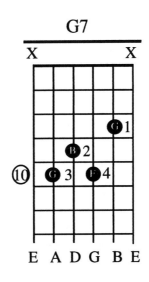
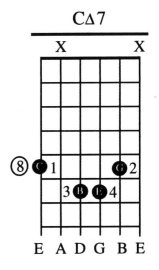

Root Position Dominant 7th sus4 Chords

Possible chord tones for C7sus4

1,4,5,b7

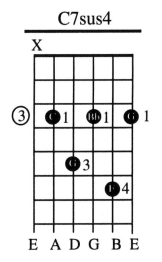

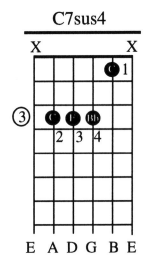

Root Position Dominant 7th sus4 Chords

Possible chord tones for C7sus4
1,4,5,b7

C7sus4

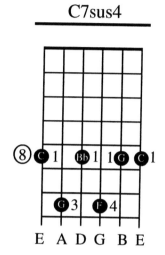

C7sus4

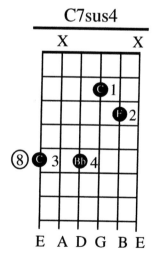

35

Root Position Minor 7b5 Chords

Possible chord tones for C-7b5

1,b3,b5,b7

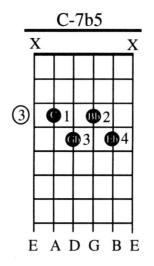

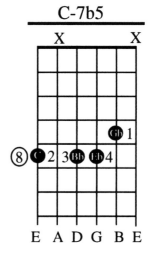

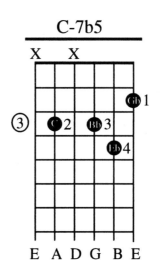

36

Chord progressions for practice

Another very common II-V-I progression is the II-V-I for a minor key. This would consist of a II -7b5 to a V 7 chord to a I -7. This minor II-V-I progression again should be practiced cycle 5.

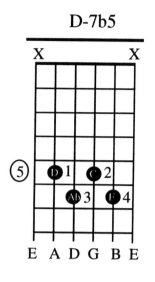

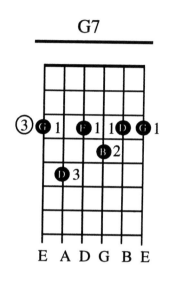

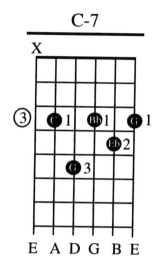

To practice this progression cycle 5 you would proceed as follows:

1. D-7b5 G7 C-7   7. Ab-7b5 Db7 Gb-7
2. G-7b5 C7 F-7   8. C#-7b5 F#7 B-7
3. C-7b5 F7 Bb-7   9. F#-7b5 B7 E-7
4. F-7b5 Bb7 Eb-7   10. B-7b5 E7 A-7
5. Bb-7b5 Eb7 Ab-7   11. E-7b5 A7 D-7
6. Eb-7b5 Ab7 Db-7   12. A-7b5 D7 G-7

Another possible way of playing this minor II-V-I progression is listed below. Make sure to learn the all the other ways of combining the II -7b5, V dom7 to I -7.

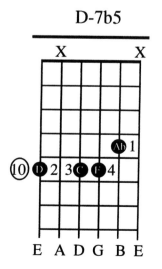

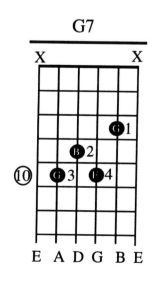

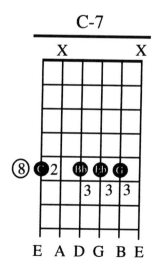

Root Position Diminished 7th Chords

Possible chord tones for C°7
1,b3,b5,bb7

*

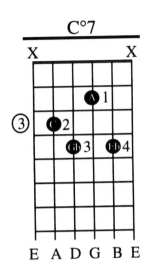

C°7

E A D G B E

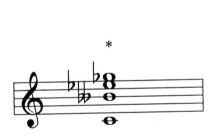

*

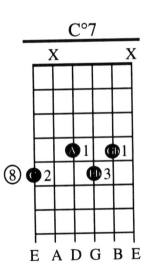

C°7

E A D G B E

* The (♭♭) sign indicates the pitch is to be lowered 2 half steps. This symbol is called a double flat.

Root Position Minor Major 7th Chords

Possible chord tones for C-Δ7

1,b3,5,7

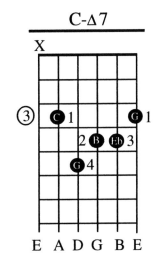

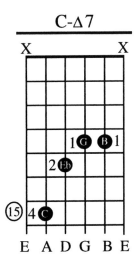

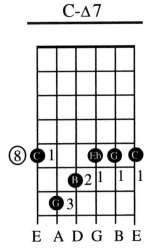

Root Position Major 7#11 Chords

Possible chord tones for CΔ7#11

1,3,#4,7

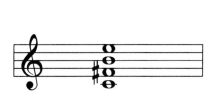

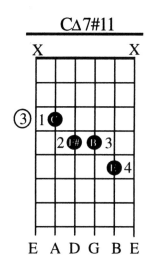

CΔ7#11

E A D G B E

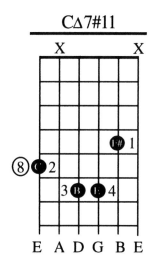

CΔ7#11

E A D G B E

Root Position Major 7th #5 Chords

Possible chord tones for CΔ7#5

1,3,#5,7

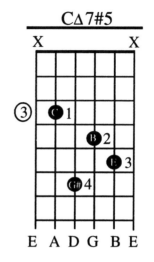

CΔ7#5

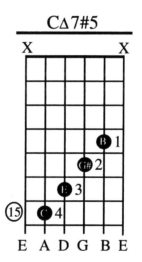

CΔ7#5

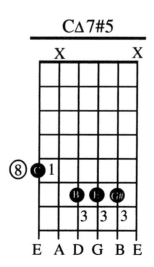

CΔ7#5

41

Root Position Dominant 7#11 Chords

Possible chord tones for C7#11
1,3,#4,b7

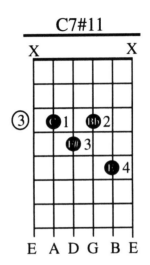

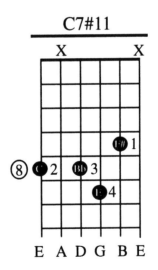

Root Position Dominant 7#5 Chords

Possible chord tones for C7#5
1,3,#5,b7

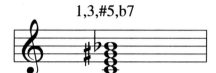

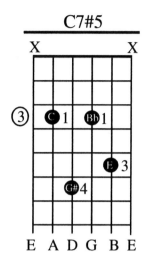

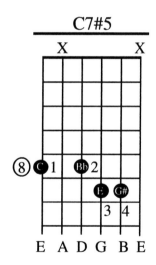

Root Position Major 6th Chords

Possible chord tones for C6

1,3,5,6

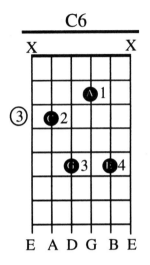

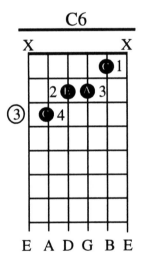

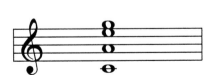

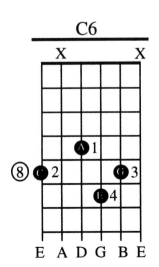

44

Root Position Minor 6th Chords

Possible chord tones for C-6

1,b3,5,6

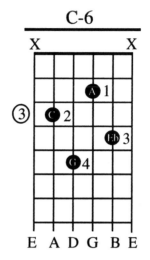

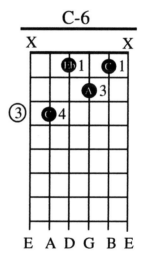

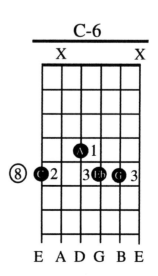

Chord progressions for practice

There are many possible combinations for II V I's using the moveable chords you have learned so far. The most common substitutions are as follows. The -7 chord can be replaced with -7b5, the 7 can be replaced with 7#11 or 7#5 and the Δ7 can be replaced with Δ7#11 Δ7#5 or 6. If the I chord is minor it can be replaced with -Δ7, or -6.

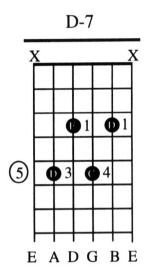

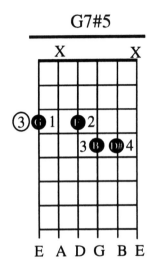

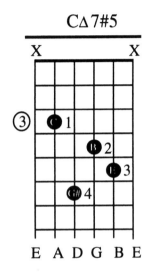

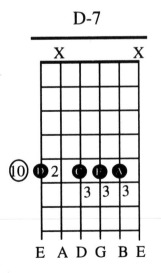

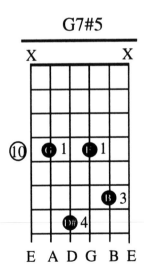

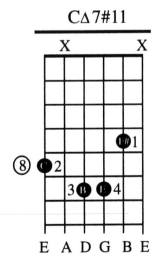

Chord progressions for practice

D-7b5
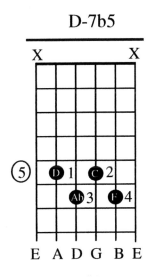

G7#5
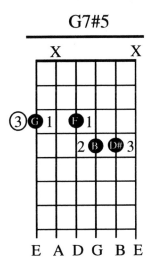

C-6
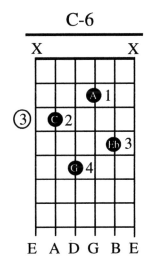

D-7b5
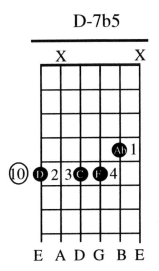

G7#11
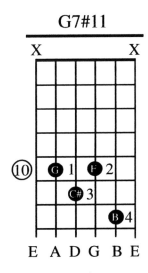

C-Δ7
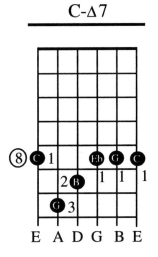

Try these progressions and other combinations as well. As we add in the tensions in the next section you will find you have thousands of possible combinations to choose from.

Chord Tones and Tensions
Major 7th
Δ7
Chord Tones 1 3 5 7
Tensions 9 #11 13

Chords with Tensions

As has been previously discussed "tensions" can be added to chords to give them more "color". Before each chord type is shown the possible tensions for that chord will be given. There is no limit to how many tensions can be in a chord but because the guitar has only 6 strings we are limited to 6 notes. Many times certain chord tones are dropped out so more tension can be placed in the chord. It is very common to drop out the 1 and 5 of the chord in order to add more tensions. As you learn each chord, notice which notes are present in each chord.

The chord tones and tensions for CΔ7 are as follows:

All the tensions that we learn for each chord can be used as a substitute for the basic chord type. For instance if we have a C chord we could substitute CΔ7 or CΔ79 etc. Theoretically this will work but you must use your ear to decide whether the sound is appropriate for the chords before and after it, and for the style of music you are playing.

Root Position Major 79 Chords

Possible chord tones and tensions for CΔ79

1,3,5,7,9

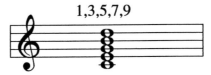

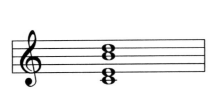

CΔ79

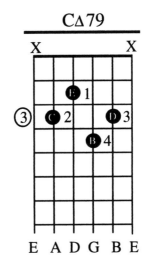

CΔ79

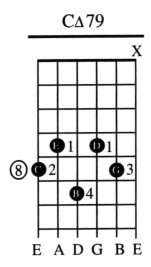

49

Root Position Major 76 Chords

Possible chord tones and tensions for C∆76

1,3,5,7,13

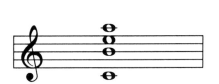

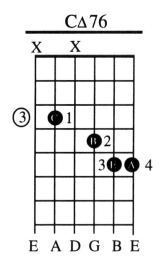

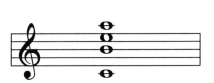

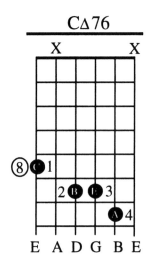

Root Position Major 79#11 Chords

Possible chord tones and tensions for CΔ79#11

1,3,#4,7,9,

CΔ79#11

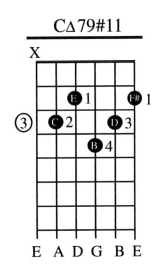

CΔ79#11

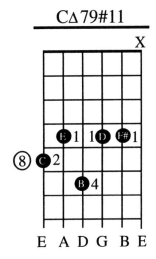

Root Position Major 769 Chord
Possible chord tones and tensions for CΔ769
1,3,5,7,9,13

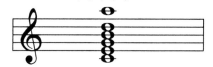

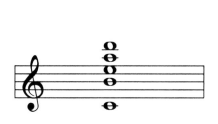

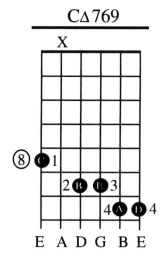

Root Position Major 769#11 Chord
Possible chord tones and tensions for CΔ769#11
1,3,#4,7,9,13

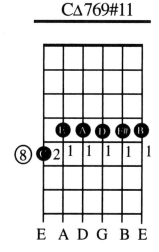

52

Root Position Major 69 Chords
Possible chord tones and tensions for C69
1,3,5,6,9

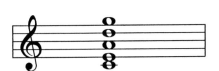

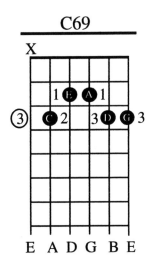

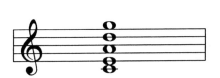

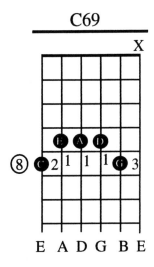

Root Position Major 69#11 Chords

Possible chord tones and tensions for C69#11

1,3,#4,6,9

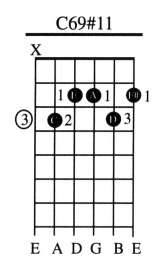

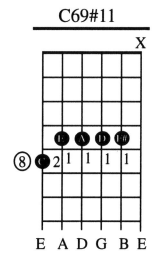

54

Root Position Major add 9 Chords
Possible chord tones and tensions for Cadd9
1,5,9

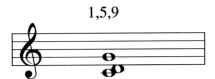

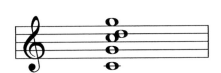

Cadd9

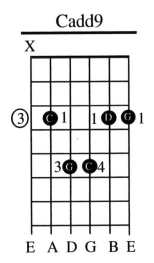

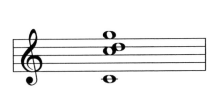

Cadd9

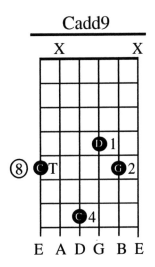

Chord Tones and Tensions
Minor 7th
-7
Chord Tones 1 b3 5 b7
Tensions 9 11 13

Chords with Tensions

Below is a list of the chord tones and tensions for a minor 7th chord. When used in a jazz context it is common to add tensions to the -7 to give it more "color". When used in a jazz tune the minor 7th chord can sound fine if it is used without tensions. This is especially true when it is the II chord of a II V I progression; however if a minor 7th is the I minor, a minor chord that is part of a vamp, or is in a ballad it is more common to add tensions.

The chord tones and tensions for C-7 are as follows:

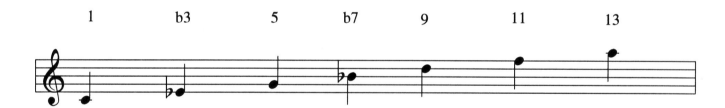

Be careful when adding tensions to a minor chord especially when adding the 9th. Sometimes the 9th can conflict, especially when the minor chord is build on the 3rd degree of a key. As always you must use your ear to decide whether the added tension is appropriate and if it sounds good with the chords before and after it. Again, different styles will affect which tensions sound the best.

Root Position Minor 9th Chords

Possible chord tones and tensions for C-9
1,b3,5,b7,9

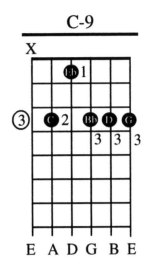

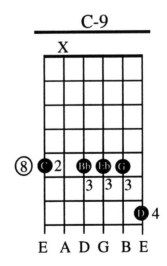

57

Root Position Minor 911 Chords

Possible chord tones and tensions for C-911
1,b3,5,b7,9,11

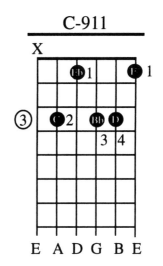

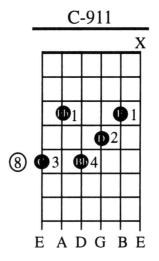

Root Position Minor 69 Chords
Possible Chord tones and tensions for C-69
1,b3,5,6,9

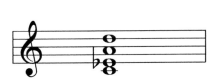

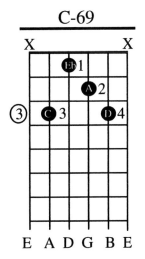

C-69

E A D G B E

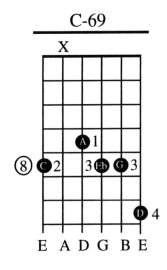

C-69

E A D G B E

59

Root Position Minor 6911 Chords

Possible chord tones and tensions for C-6911

1,b3,5,6,9,11

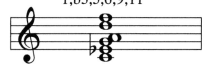

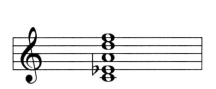

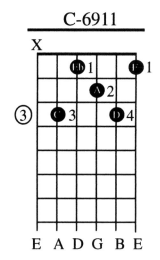

C-6911

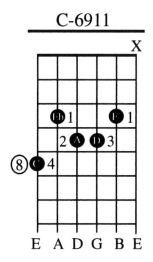

C-6911

Root Position Minor 11th Chords

Possible chord tones and tensions for C-11

1,b3,5,b7,11

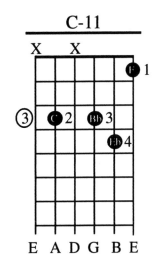

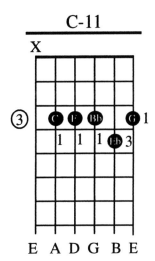

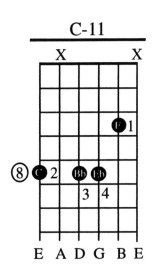

Root Position Minor 6 11 Chords

Possible chord tones and tensions for C-611

1,b3,5,6,11

C-611

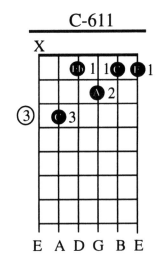

C-611

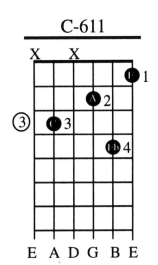

C-611

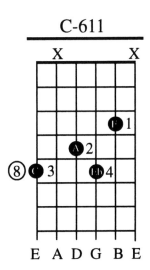

Root Position Minor 6 7 Chords*

Possible chord tones and tensions for C-67

1,b3,5,6,b7

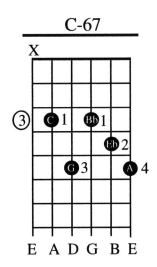

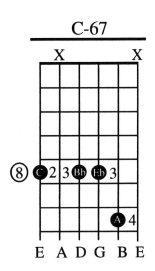

* C-67 could also be called a C-7(13).

Chord Tones and Tensions
Dominant 7th
7
Chord Tones 1 3 5 b7
Tensions b9 9 #9 #11 #5 13

Chords with Tensions

Below is a list of the chord tones and tensions for a dominant chord.   There is no limit to how many tensions can be in a chord, but because the guitar has only 6 strings we are limited to 6 notes.

The chord tones and tensions for C7 are as follows:

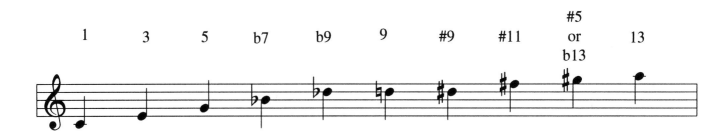

All the tensions that we learn for each chord can be used as a substitute for the basic chord type. Dominant chords have many possibilities for adding and combining tensions. For instance if we have a C7 chord we could substitute C7#11 or C7#9b13 etc. Theoretically any combination is possible. Usually tensions are not combined that are a half step apart. For example, you usually don't have a dominant chord which contains "b9" and natural 9. Also most of these half step possibilities make for difficult and awkward playing on the guitar.

Although any tension combination is possible, there are common situations where certain tensions are preferred over others. When a dominant chord resolves up a fourth to a major chord i.e. C7 to FΔ7 it is common to use natural tensions 9 or 13. When a dominant chord resolves up a fourth to a minor chord i.e. C7 to F-7 it is common to use the altered tensions b9, #9, #11, b13. The reason C7 to FΔ7 uses natural tension is that the 9 and 13 (in this case, on C7 that would be D and A), are diatonic to the F major scale therefore creating an expectation of an impending major resolution. On the other hand if C7 resolves to an F minor chord, the altered tensions (in this case, on C7 they would be Db, Eb, Ab) are commonly used because they are found in various F minor scales. Db and Ab could be from the F harmonic minor scale and Eb from the natural minor scale. There are of course many other F minor scales that these three notes are found in. You can find many examples of these different tension combinations in the progression section found at the end of this book.

Root Position Dominant 9 Chords

Possible chord tones and tensions for C9

1,3,5,b7,9

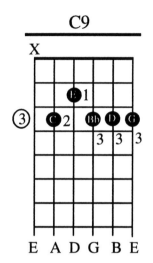

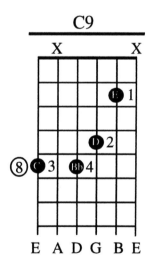

Root Position Dominant 7b9 Chords
Possible chord tones and tensions for C7b9
1,3,5,b7,b9

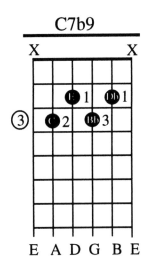

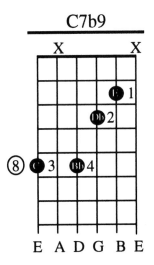

Root Position Dominant 7#9 Chords

Possible chord tones and tensions for C7#9

1,3,5,b7,#9

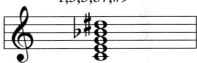

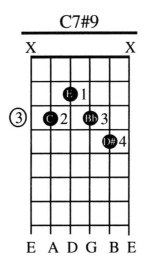

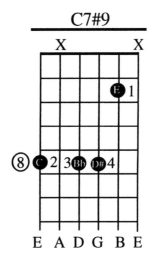

Root Position Dominant 13th Chords

Possible chord tones and tensions for C13

1,3,5,b7,13

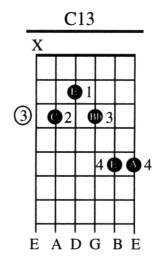

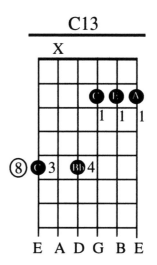

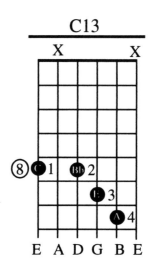

Chord Progressions

Below are listed a few chord progressions using the 13th and 9th chords for the dominant. Practice these progressions cycle 5

D-7

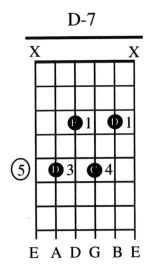

G13

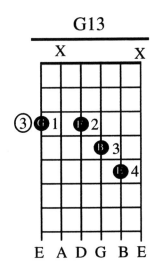

CΔ7

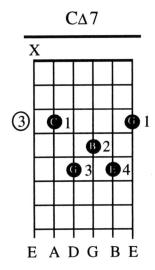

D-7

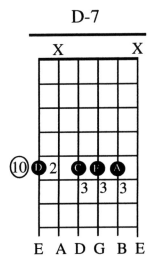

G9

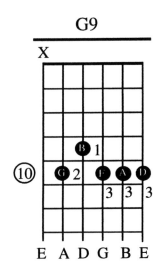

CΔ7

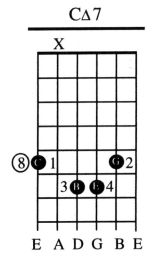

Root Position Dominant 7b13 Chords *

Possible chord tones and tensions for C7b13
1,3,5,** b7,b13

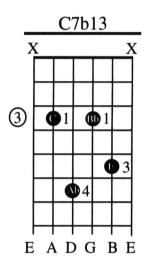

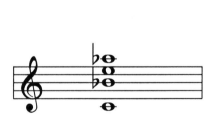

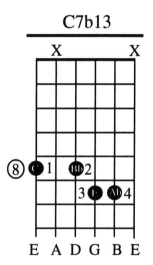

*C7b13 has the same notes as C7#5

** The 5th of the chord is commonly omitted on a 7b13 and is never used on a 7#5 chord.

Root Position Dominant 913 Chords

Possible chord tones and tensions for C913

1,3,5,b7,9,13

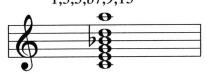

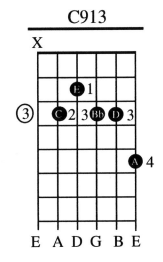

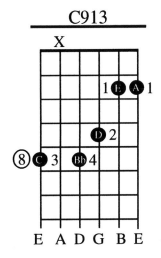

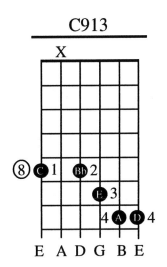

Root Position Dominant 9b13 Chords

Possible chord tones for C9b13

1,3,5,b7,9,b13

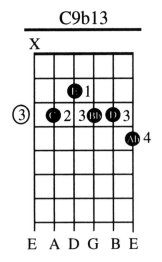

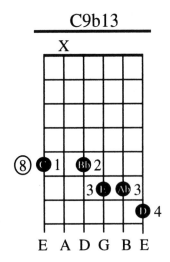

72

Root Position Dominant 7b913 Chords

Possible chord tones and tensions for C7b913

1,3,5,b7,b9,13

C7b913

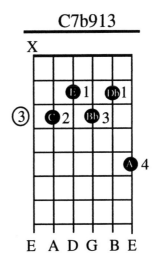

C7b913

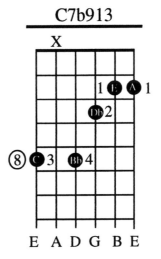

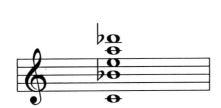

C7b913

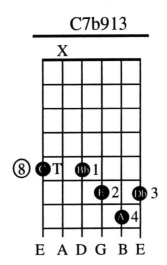

Root Position Dominant 7#913 Chords

Possible chord tones and tensions for C7#913
1,3,5,b7,#9,13

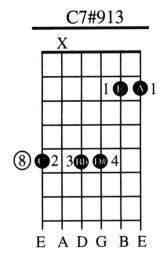

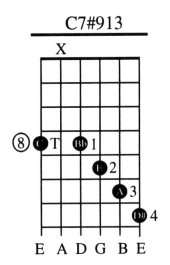

Root Position Dominant 7b9b13 Chords

Possible chord tones and tensions for C7b9b13

1,3,5,b7,b9,b13

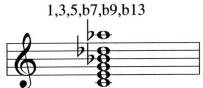

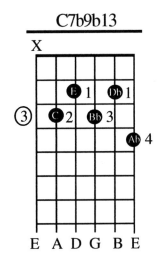

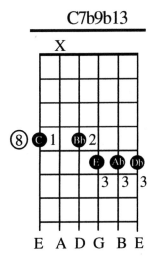

75

Root Position Dominant 7#9b13 Chords

Possible chord tones and tensions for C7#9b13

1,3,5,b7,#9,b13

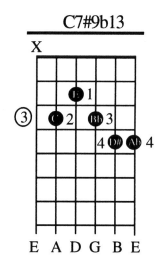

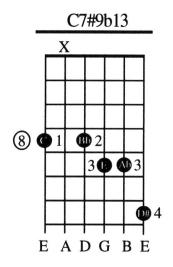

Root Position Dominant 9#11 Chords

Possible chord tones and tensions for C9#11
1,3,#4,b7,9,

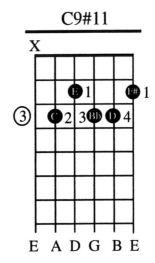

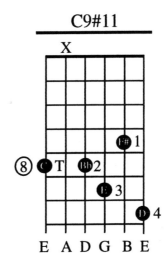

Root Position Dominant 7b9#11 Chords

Possible chord tones and tensions for C7b9#11

1,3,#4,b7,b9

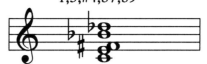

C7b9#11

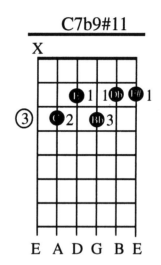

E A D G B E

C7b9#11

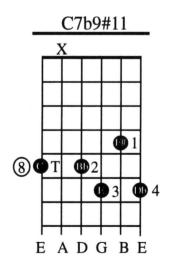

E A D G B E

Root Position Dominant 7#9#11 Chords

Possible Chord tones and tensions for C7#9#11

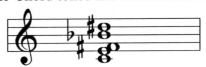

C7#9#11

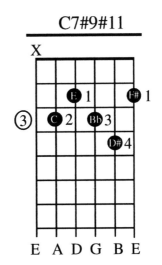

C7#9#11

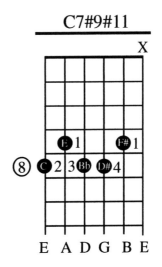

Chord progressions for practice

Below are listed a few chord progression using the chords containing tensions. These II-V-I progression should be practiced cycle 5.

D-7
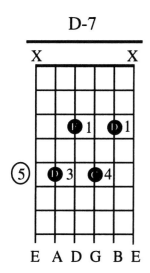

G7b13
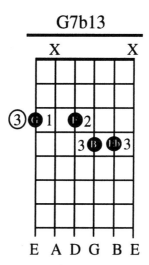

C69
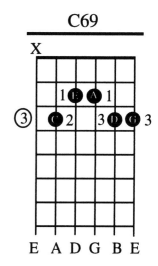

D-7
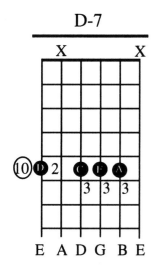

G7b9
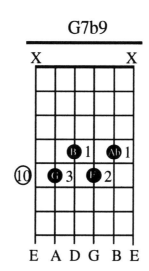

C6
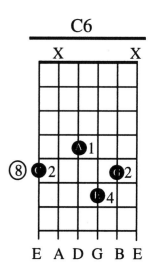

Chord progressions for practice

D-9

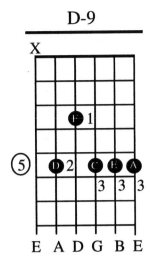

G7b9b13

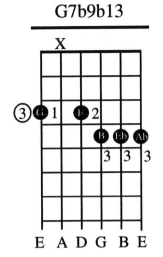

C69#11

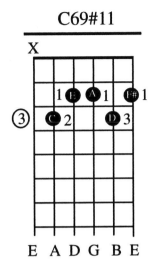

D-11

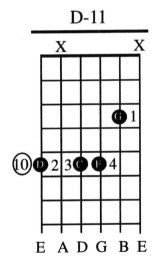

G7#9b13

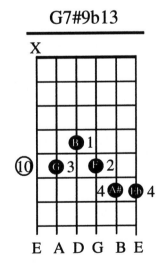

CΔ76#11

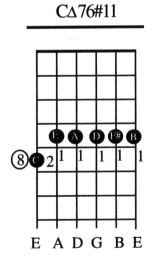

81

Chord progressions for practice

D-911

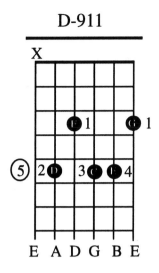

G7#9b13

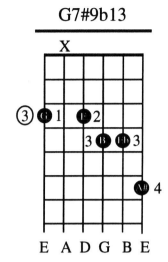

C-69

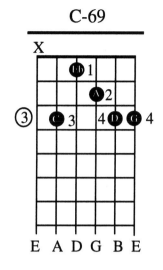

D-11

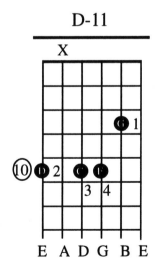

G7#9#11

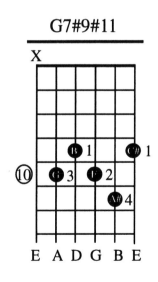

C-679

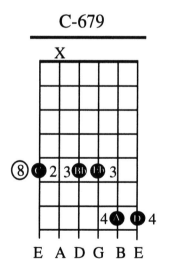

82

Chord progressions for practice

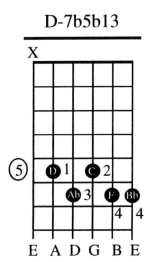

D-7b5b13

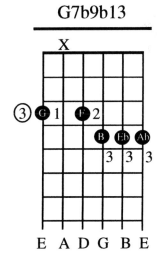

G7b9b13

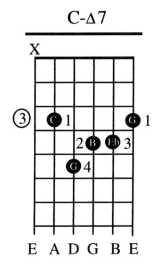

C-Δ7

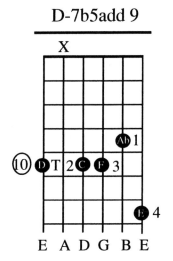

D-7b5add 9

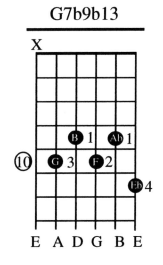

G7b9b13

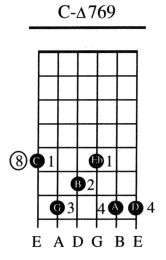

C-Δ769

Chord Tones and Tensions
Dominant 7th sus4
7sus4
Chord Tones 1 4 5 b7
Tensions b9 9 #9 10 b13 13

Chords with Tensions

Below is a list of the chord tones and tensions for a dominant 7th sus4 chord. Dominant 7th sus4 is commonly found in jazz where there is a vamp or when it is placed before a dominant 7th. For example, C7sus4 to C7.   Like the minor 7th chord the 7sus4 chord can sound fine if it is used without tensions.

The chord tones and tensions for C7sus4 are as follows:

Many of the voicings of the dominant 7sus4 chords on guitar contain a lot of 4th intervals. This creates a very "open" sound and is commonly used for vamps. It is also common to use the 7sus4 voicing as a vehicle to slide in and out of a key center by moving the chord up and down a half step or to other intervals. You could easily take the E minor blues progression on page 117 and substitute 7sus4 chords to create a nice open harmonic adventurous sound.

Root Position Dominant 9sus4 Chords

Possible chord tones and tensions for C9sus4

1,4,5,b7,9

C9sus4

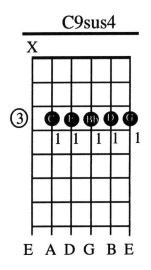

C9sus4

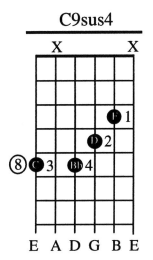

C9sus4

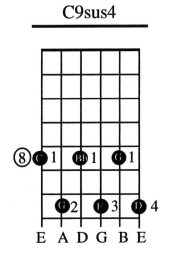

Root Position Dominant 7sus4b9 Chords

Possible chord tones and tensions for C7sus4b9

1,4,5,b7,b9

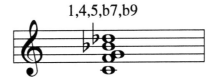

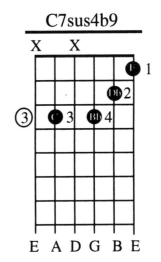

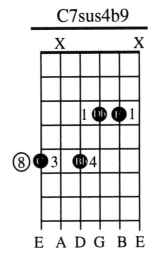

Root Position Dominant 9sus4add13 Chord

Possible chord tones and tensions for C9sus4add13

1,4,5,b7,9,13

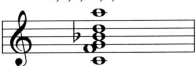

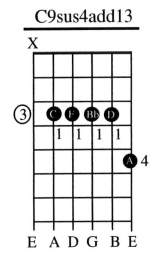

Root Position Dominant 13sus4 Chord

Possible chord tones and tensions for C13sus4

1,4,5,b7,13

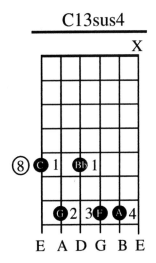

Root Position Dominant 7sus4#913 Chords

Possible chord tones and tensions for C7sus4#913

1,4,5,b7,#9,13

C7sus4#913

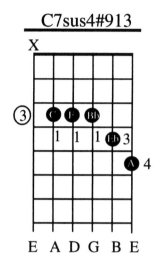

C7sus4#913

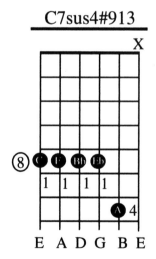

Root Position Dominant 7sus4#9b13 Chords

Possible chord tones and tensions for C7sus4#9b13

1,4,5,b7,#9,b13

C7sus4#9b13

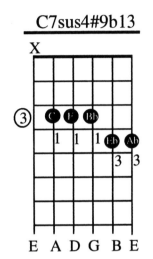

C7sus4#9b13

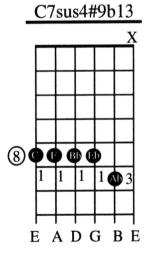

Root Position Dominant 13sus4 add 10 Chords

Possible chord tones and tensions for C7sus13add10
1,4,5,b7,10,13

C13sus4 add 10

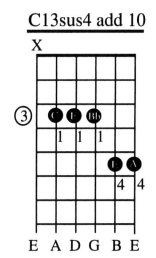

C13sus4 add 10

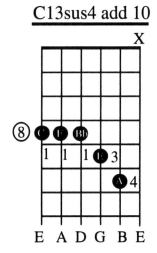

Root Position Dominant 7sus4b9#9b13 Chord

Possible chord tones and tensions for C7sus4b9#9b13

1,4,5,b7,b9,#9,b13

C7sus4b9#9b13

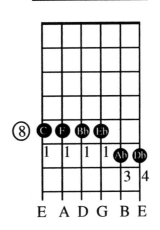

Chord Tones and Tensions
Minor 7th flat 5
-7b5
Chord Tones 1 b3 b5 b7
Tensions 9 11 b13

Chords with Tensions

Below is a list of the chord tones and tensions for a minor 7b5 chord.   Minor 7b5 is commonly found in jazz as a II chord in a II V I of minor. For example, D-7b5 to G7b9 to C-7. Like the minor 7th chord the -7b5 chord can sound fine if it is used without tensions. Because of the fingering difficulty associated with adding tensions to a -7b5 chord, guitarists frequently don't add in tensions when playing this chord. The tensions do create a great sound when the situation allows, so don't be afraid to experiment.

The chord tones and tensions for -7b5 are as follows:

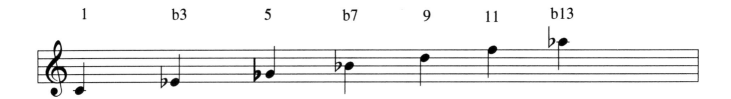

Root Position Minor 7b5add9 Chord

Possible chord tones and tensions for C-7b5add9

1,b3,b5,b7,9

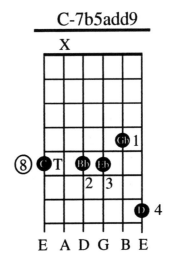

C-7b5add9

Root Position Minor 7b5b13 Chord

Possible chord tones and tensions for C-7b5b13

1,b3,b5,b7,b13

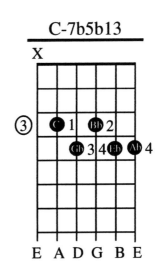

C-7b5b13

93

Chord Tones and Tensions
Diminished 7th
°7
Chord Tones 1 b3 b5 bb7
Tensions 9 11 b13 b15

Chords with Tensions

Below is a list of the chord tones and tensions for a diminished 7th chord.   °7 is commonly found in jazz as a passing chord. For example, CΔ7 to C#°7 to D-7. You will also find the °7 as a I diminished chord. For example, CΔ7 to C°7 to CΔ7.   Like the minor 7th chord the °7 chord can sound fine if it is used without tensions. Because of the fingering difficulty associated with adding tensions to a °7 chord guitarist frequently don't add them in when playing this chord. Tensions do create a great sound when the situation allows, so don't be afraid to experiment.

The chord tones and tensions for °7 are as follows:

Root Position Diminished 7b13 Chord

Possible chord tones and tensions for °7b13
1,b3,b5,bb7,b13

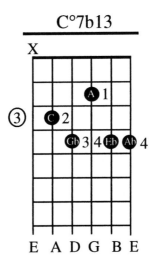

Root Position Diminished 7add Δ7 Chord

Possible chord tones and tensions for °7addΔ7
1,b3,b5,bb7,b15*

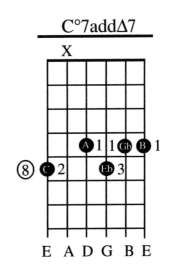

* b15 (B) is the same note as the major 7, also C°7add Δ7 has the same notes as -Δ7b5add6 (see page 98)

Chord Tones and Tensions
Minor Major 7th
-Δ7
Chord Tones 1 b3 5 7
Tensions 9 11 #11 13

Chords with Tensions

Below is a list of the chord tones and tensions for a -Δ7 chord. -Δ7 is commonly used in jazz as a substitute chord for a minor 7th. For example, rather than D-7b5 to G7b9 to C-7, you would use D-7b5 to G7b9 to C-Δ7. When a -7 chord is the last chord of a song the -Δ7 is a commonly used as a replacement. This creates a sound that really feels like the song has ended . For example if the song ends on a C-7 you could replace it with a C-Δ7. Like the minor 7th chord the -Δ7 chord can sound fine if it is used without tensions. Again, because of the fingering difficulty associated with adding tensions to a -Δ7 chord, guitarists frequently don't add in tensions when playing it. By the way, I highly recommend using the -Δ7b5 chord as an ending chord, it sounds great.

The chord tones and tensions for -Δ7 are as follows:

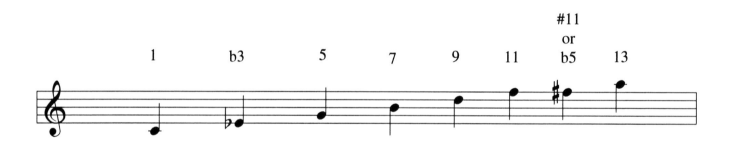

96

Root Position Minor Major 79 Chord

Possible chord tones and tensions for C-Δ79

1,b3,5,7,9

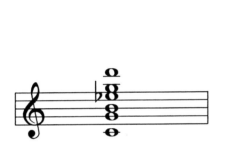

C-Δ79

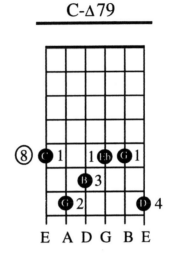

Root Position Minor Major 76 Chord

Possible chord tones and tensions for C-Δ76

1,b3,5,7,13

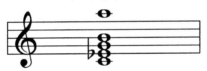

C-Δ76

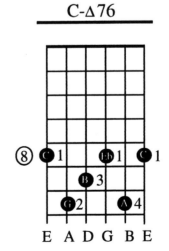

97

Root Position Minor Major 7b5 Chord

Possible chord tones and tensions for C-Δ7b5

1,b3,b5,7

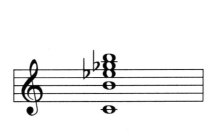

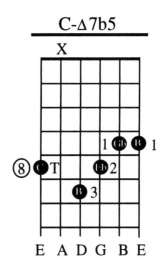

Root Position Minor Major 7b5add6 Chord*

Possible chord tones and tensions for C-Δ7b5add6

1,b3,b5,7,13

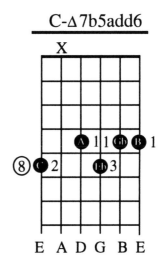

* This chord could also be a C°7addΔ7 (see page 95)

Root Position Minor Major 769 Chord

Possible Chord tones and tensions for C-Δ 769
1,b3,5,7,9,13

C-Δ769

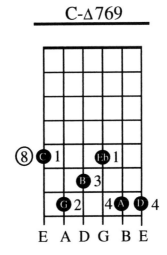

Chord Tones and Tensions
Major 7th sharp 5
Δ7#5
Chord Tones 1 3 #5 7
Tensions 9 #11

Chords with Tensions

    Below is a list of the chord tones and tensions for a Δ7#5 chord. Δ7#5 is commonly used in jazz as a substitute chord for a Δ7 chord. For example, rather than D-7 to G7 to CΔ7, you would use D-7 to G7 to CΔ7#5. When a Δ7 chord is the last chord of a song the Δ7#5 is a commonly used as a replacement. This creates a highly colorful sound that really spices up the end of a tune . For example if the song ends on a CΔ7 you could replace it with a CΔ7#5. Like the minor 7th chord, the CΔ7#5 chord can sound fine if it is used without tensions. This is another example of infrequently added tensions due to fingering difficulties. But if you can do it, the rewards are there. I highly recommend using the CΔ7#5 chord as an ending chord, it works beautifully.

The chord tones and tensions for CΔ7#5 are as follows:

Root Position Major 7#5 add9 Chord

Possible Chord tones and tensions for CΔ7#5add9

1,3,#5,7,9

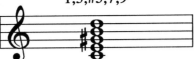

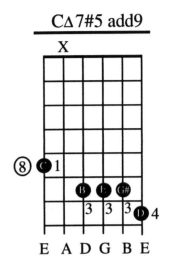

CΔ7#5 add9

Chord Progressions and Reharmonization Theory

The chord progressions found in the next section are very common in blues and jazz music. The 12 bar blues, the minor 12 bar blues and rhythm changes (a common progression in jazz music) are shown to help a student utilize all the chords found in this book. Both blues and rhythm changes are presented in all keys first with chord symbols and then with only notes. It is important for a guitarist to be able to read both chord symbols and written out voicings. Feel free to substitute chords with different tensions to create your own examples. Each progression will have many chords that can be played in different positions on the guitar; the voicings I used are shown in the "notes only" section starting on page 131. The fret position is also shown with a number inside a circle under each chord, but again, feel free to try other combinations and use your ear to decide which voicing sounds the best.

It is important to see how all the chords presented in this book fit into music. Three very common chord progressions will be shown in all 12 keys moving in a cycle 5 pattern. The first, the blues, is typically a 12 bar song form with the IV chord coming on the fifth bar. You will notice the many different ways a blues can be played by substituting all the chords we have learned. The minor blues is again a 12 bar form with the IV chord coming on the 5th measure. Rhythm Changes is a common AABA jazz form: A=8bars, A=8bars, B=8bars, A=8bars. The A sections are re-harmonized slightly to add variety. Try to learn each example at the tempo marking and make sure all the notes of each chord sound clear.

The 12 bar blues, minor blues, and rhythm changes are all basic progression that are then embellished with more chords and/or tensions. Pages 103 and 104 show the stripped down versions of the 12 Bar Blues, Minor Blues and Rhythm Changes. The 12 Bar Blues and the Minor Blues (see page 103) are similar in that they go to the IV chord (IV in the Key of C) on the fifth measure. You will notice that even when reharmonizations get very complex usually the IV chord will still be there on the 5th measure. Rhythm changes as mentioned before have an AABA form, therefore there are only two sections to the form; the A section consists of a diatonic progression in C (C, A-, D-, G7) or I, VI, II, V, with a quick II-V-I to the IV chord G-7 C7 F which is another II, V, I but in F major, then another I, VI, II, V, in C. This is followed by a bridge (B section) which goes through dominant 7th chords cycle 5: E7 to A7 to D7 to G7.

With this basic information we can now talk about the reharmonization I have added to these basic progressions. One method of reharmonization is to add and subtract tensions. By referring to the chord tones and tensions chart presented before each chord type you can add any of the available tensions. Therefore C Major could be C69 because 6 and 9 are available tensions for a C chord. Another method involves adding and subtracting chords to change the chord progression. Reharmonization by adding and subtracting chords has certain rules that govern which chords are substituted. This reharmonization theory is derived from the fact that our ear wants certain types of chords to resolve in certain ways and that some chords have an affinity with others because of their internal structure. A chord's tendency to move in a particular way is called its " resolution tendency." One chord with a very strong resolution tendency is the dominant chord. Our ear wants to hear the dominant chord resolve in one of 3 ways: up a 4th (G7 to CΔ7), down a half step (Db7 to CΔ7), or up a whole step (Bb7 to CΔ7). These resolution tendencies of the dominant are also listed in order of the strongest resolution to the weakest. Therefore G7 to CΔ7 is the strongest and Bb7 to CΔ7 is the weakest. With this information we can take a blues and put the corresponding dominant structure before any chord. This dominant will then create a resolution to the chord that follows. The first example of the 12 bar blues (page 107) does this in the 4th bar. You have an F#9 chord resolving down a half step to F9 in the 5th bar, then in bar 6 you have Bb13 resolving up a whole step to C13. To review, we have **3 resolutions for a dominant chord, up a 4th, down a half step, or up a whole step**. Thinking of this another way if we have CΔ7 we could put G7, Db7 or Bb7 in front of it for three possible reharmonizations.

The 12 Bar Blues

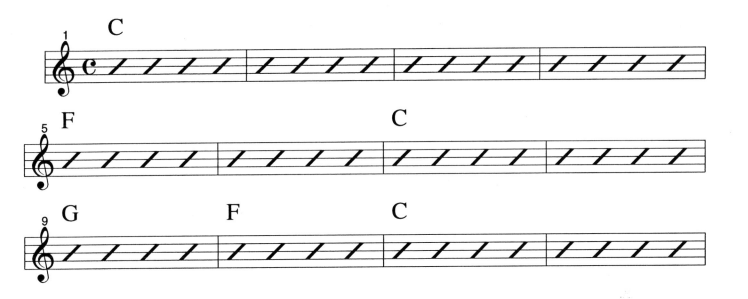

The Minor Blues

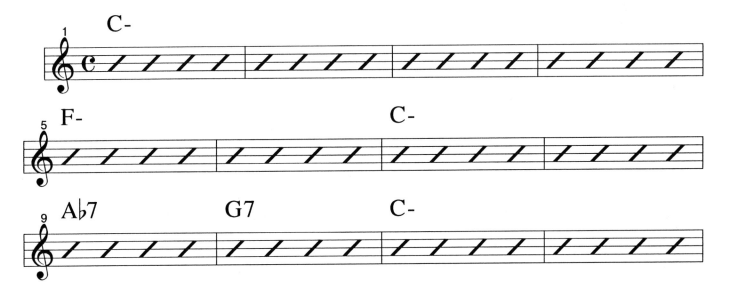

Rhythm Changes

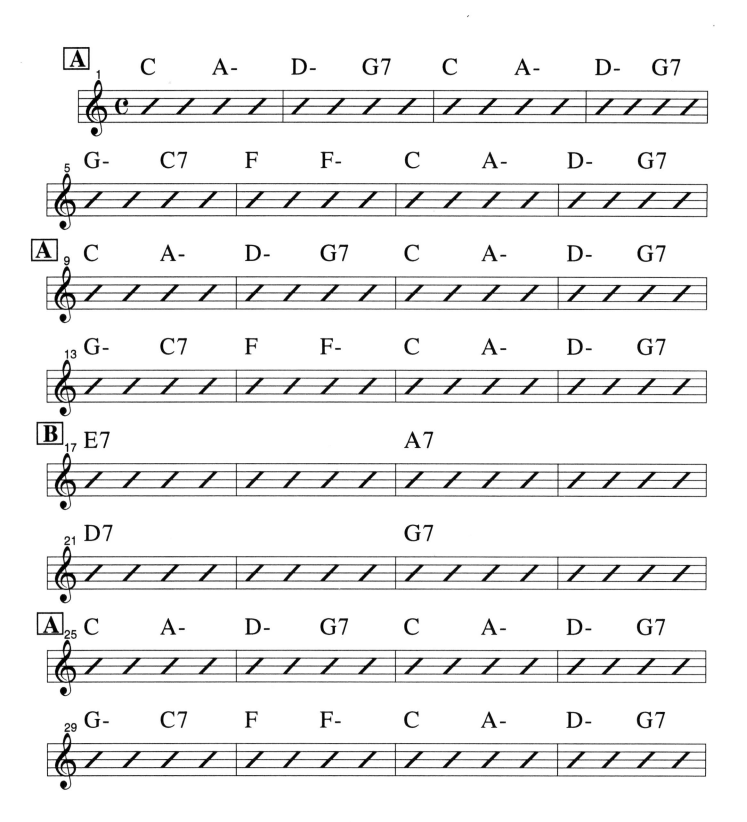

Another common substitution is to place the related II -7 in front of the 7th chord. For example if you have G7 to CΔ7 you can substitute D-7 to G7 to CΔ7 or II-V-I. Using this idea we can use the -7 in front of our other two resolutions of the dominant Ab-7 to Db7 to CΔ7 and F-7 to Bb7 to CΔ7. Again these are listed in the order of strongest to weakest

An example of this can be seen on page 107 with the 12 Bar Blues progression in F (bottom example). The D-7 in bar 8 resolves to the G7b13 in bar 9 which then resolves to the C13 in bar 10. Check out the chord progressions to find more examples of this substitution. We can extend this theory to get even more possibilities for substitution. If CΔ7 can have 3 possible dominant chords: G7, Db7 and Bb7, **then these three dominants can be freely substituted for each other**. A progression of G7 to CΔ7 can just as well be Db7 to CΔ7 or Bb7 to CΔ7; you just have to keep in mind that some dominant resolutions are stronger than others. If we continue with this idea **all the -7's that can precede the dominant 7'th can be freely substituted for each other**. Below is a list of all the possibilities starting from strongest to weakest.

D-7 G7 CΔ7	Ab-7 Db7 CΔ7	F-7 Bb7 CΔ7	Strongest
D-7 Db7 CΔ7	Ab-7 G7 CΔ7	F-7 G7 CΔ7	↓
D-7 Bb7 CΔ7	Ab-7 Bb7 CΔ7	F-7 Db7 CΔ7	Weakest

An example of this type of substitution can be found on page 107. The 12 Bar Blues progression in F (bottom example) has a C-7 resolving to B13 in the 4th measure. This B13 then resolves to Bb13 in the 5th measure. You will find hundreds of examples of these substitutions throughout the chord progression section of this book.

Chords are also substituted because their internal structure is very similar. The most common example of this is the substitutions that occur within the diatonic chords of a key. If we look at the diatonic chords of C major we can see that CΔ7, E-7 and A-7 all have many notes in common. D-7 and FΔ7 also have many notes in common as does G7 and B-7b5. Our ear picks up on this and doesn't mind if we substitute these similar structures.

Diatonic 7th chords of C major

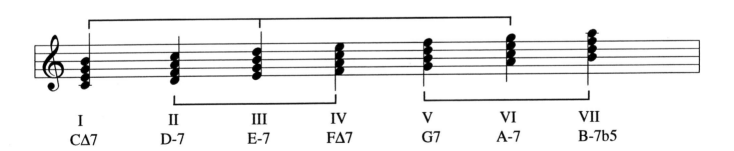

I	II	III	IV	V	VI	VII
CΔ7	D-7	E-7	FΔ7	G7	A-7	B-7b5

These three different groups of chords are commonly referred to as the tonic area (CΔ7, E-7 and A-7), the subdominant area (D-7 and FΔ7) and the dominant area (G7 and B-7b5). You will find many examples of this type of substitution in the rhythm changes progressions. For example on page 119 in the 3rd bar E-7 is substituted for CΔ7.

If we extend this idea further we can find other chords that have a lot of notes in common and use those for substitutions. For example the D#°7 chord in bar 10 of the Rhythm changes in C (page 119) has the notes D#, F#, A, and C. If we look at the chord in the next measure (measure 11) we see it is an E-7. We have learned that E-7 can be preceded by B7; the notes in B7 are B, D#, F#, A. If we compare D#°7 and B7 we find that they differ only in one note; D#°7 contains a C, and B7 contains a B. C (the b9 of B7) is an available tension on a dominant, therefore, D#°7 works as a substitution for B7. Another example of this type of substitution can be found on page 115. In measure 7 of the Minor Blues in Db (bottom example) the usual chord would have been some type of Db-. This Db- could include any of the available tensions for a minor chord (Db-7, Db-Δ7, Db-69, etc.). In place of the Db- we have a EΔ7#5. If we compare the chord tones of EΔ7#5 (E, G#, C, and D#) with the chord tones of Db-Δ9 (Db, E, Ab, C, Eb) we find that all the notes of EΔ7#5 are contained in Db-Δ9, therefore EΔ7#5 can be substituted for Db-Δ9.

The substitutions mentioned in this book are very common in all types of music. Future volumes of this chord workbook series will explore other chord substitutions and chord voicings for the guitar.

Numbers in circles below each chord refer to which fret the voicing is played on.

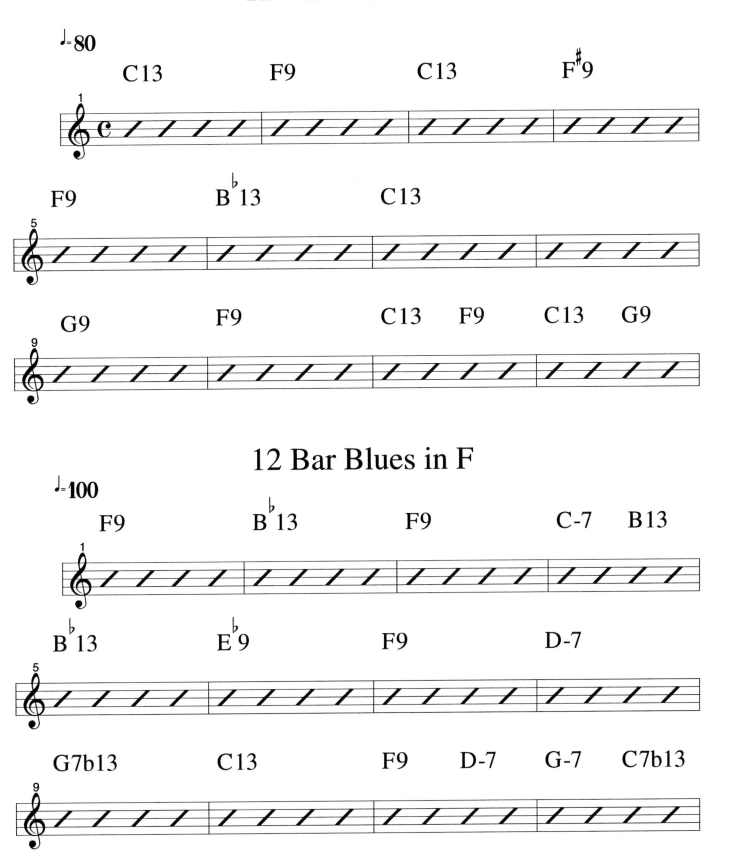

12 Bar Blues in Bb

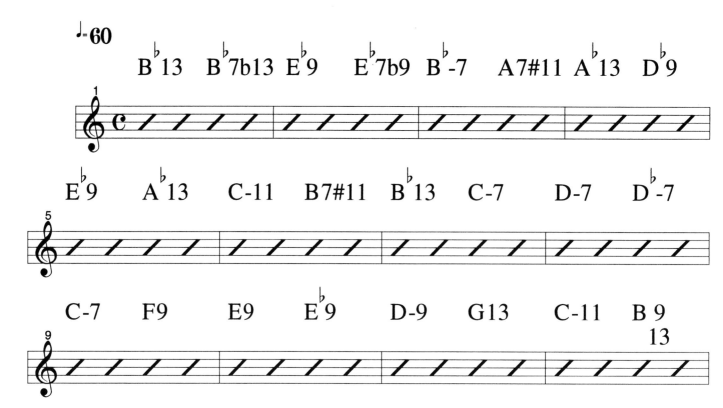

12 Bar Blues in Eb

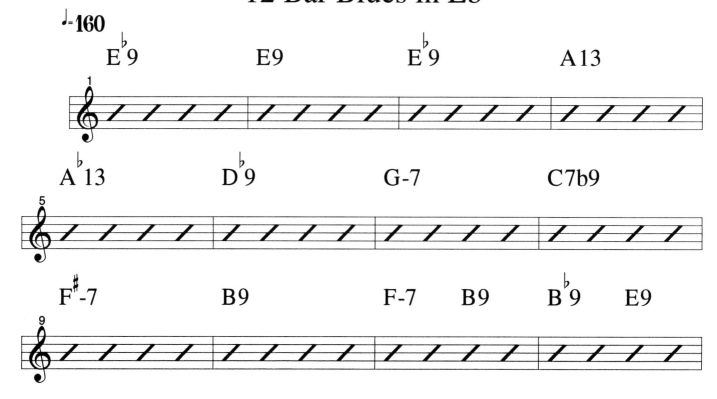

12 Bar Blues in Ab

109

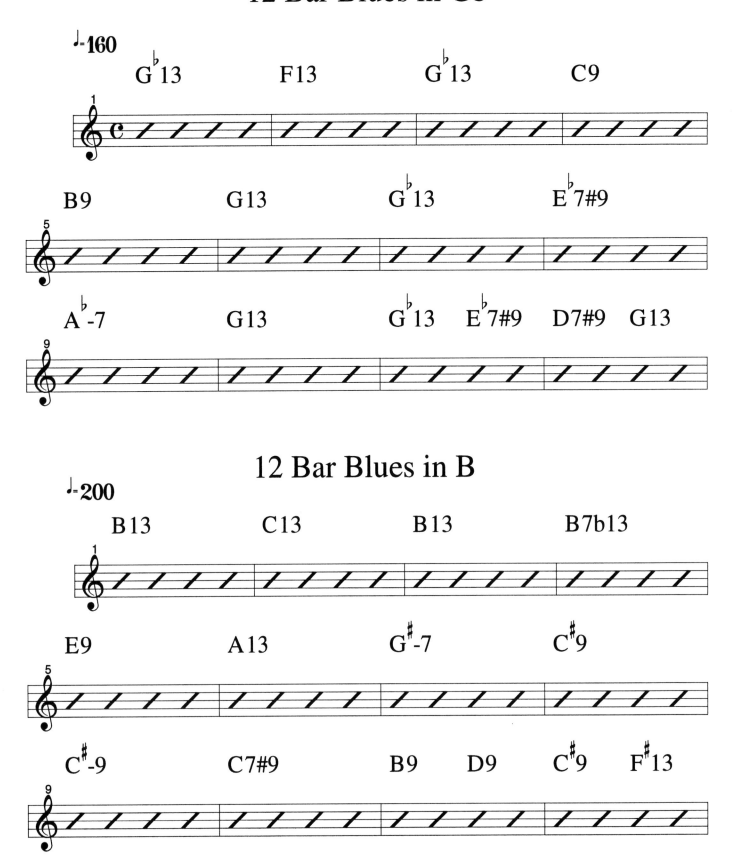

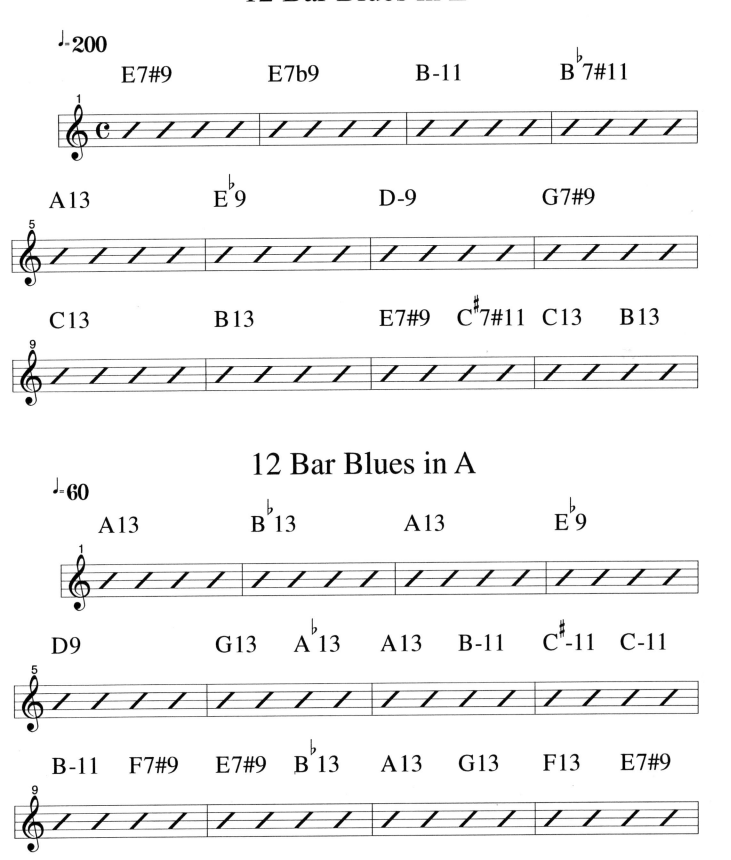

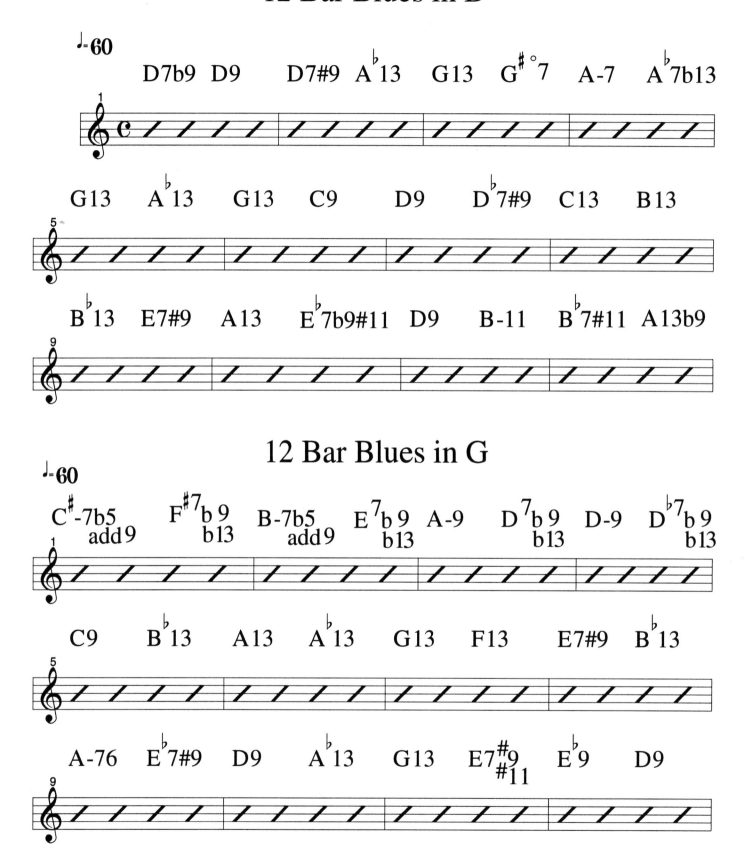

C Minor Blues

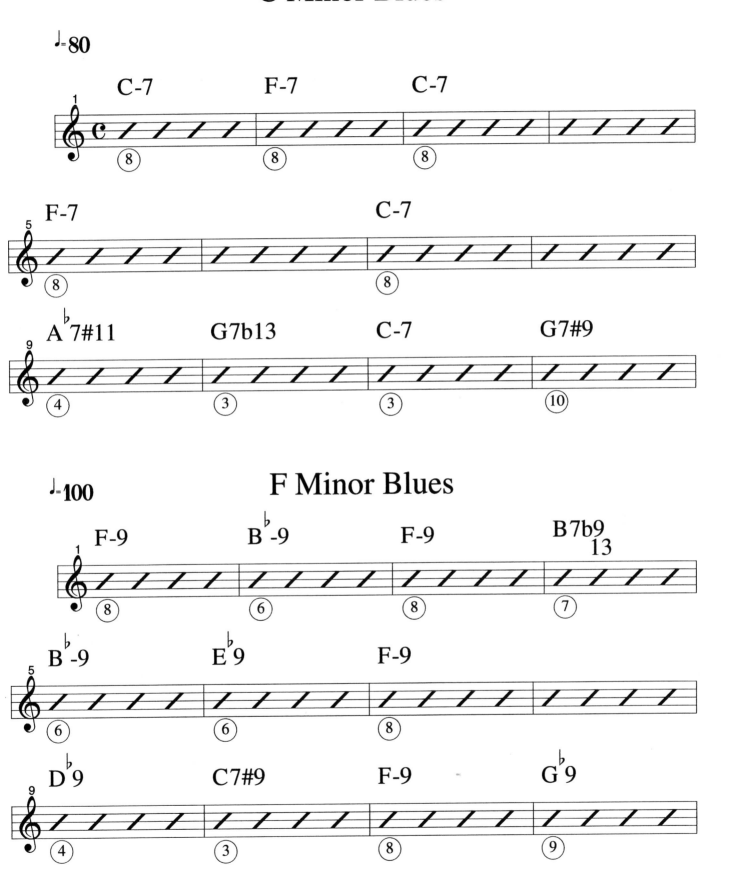

F Minor Blues

Bb Minor Blues

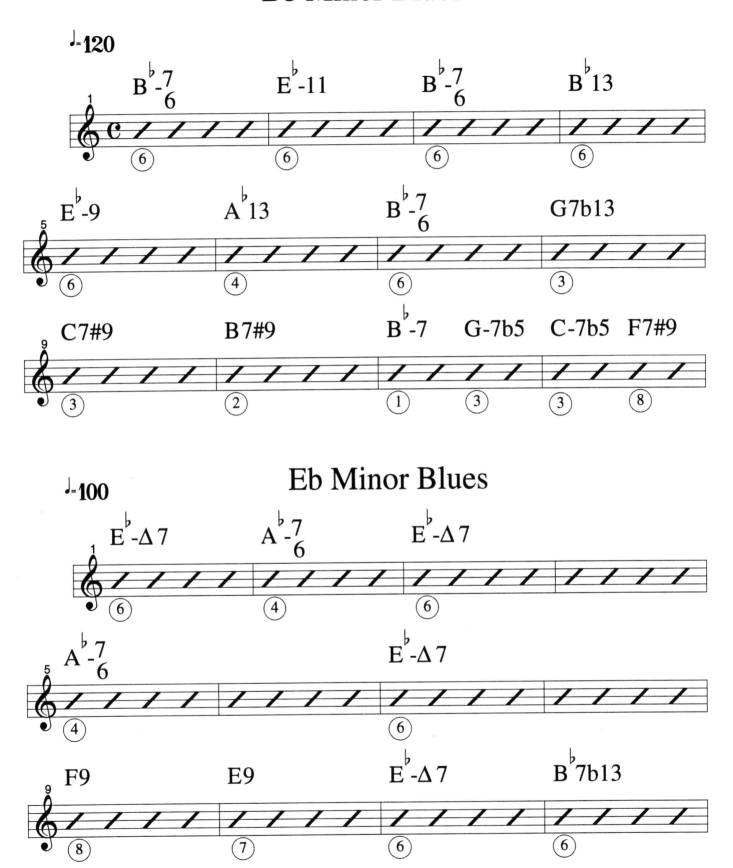

Eb Minor Blues

Ab Minor Blues

Db Minor Blues

Gb Minor Blues

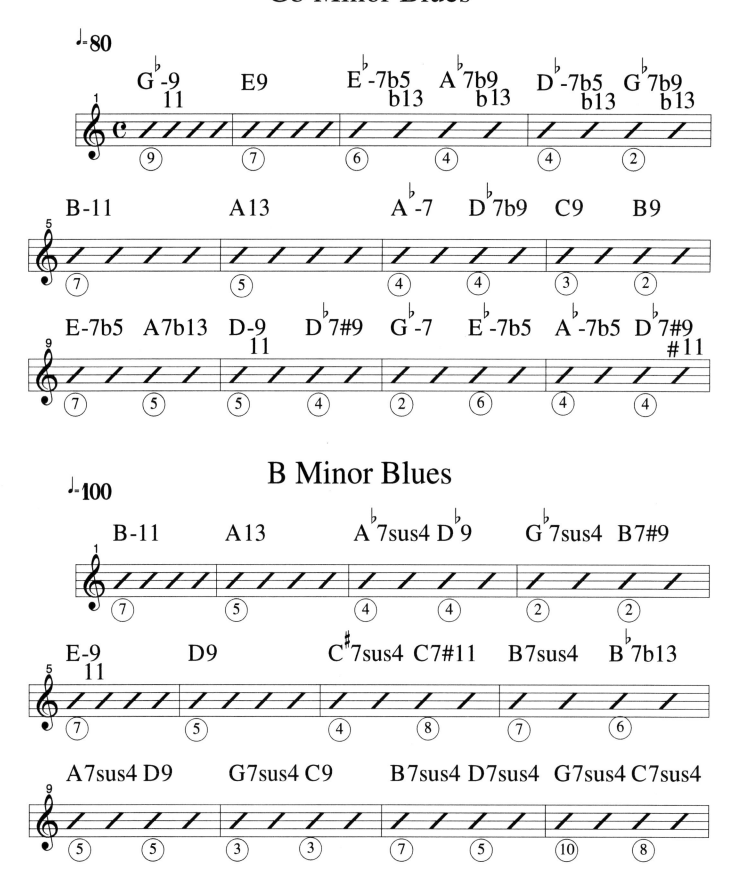

B Minor Blues

E Minor Blues

A Minor Blues

D Minor Blues

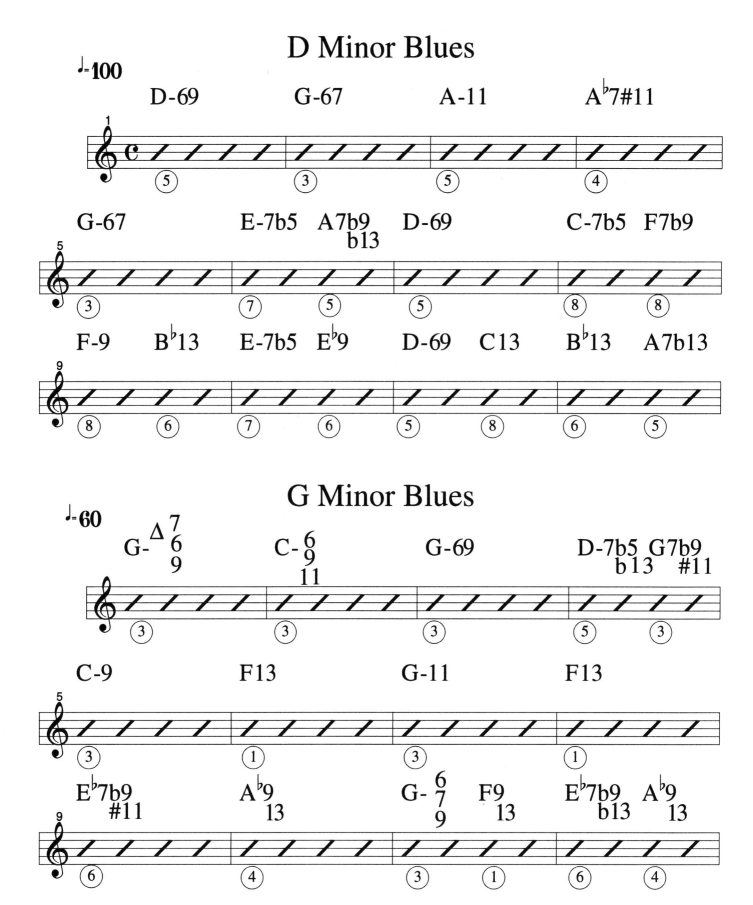

G Minor Blues

119

Rhythm Changes in F Major

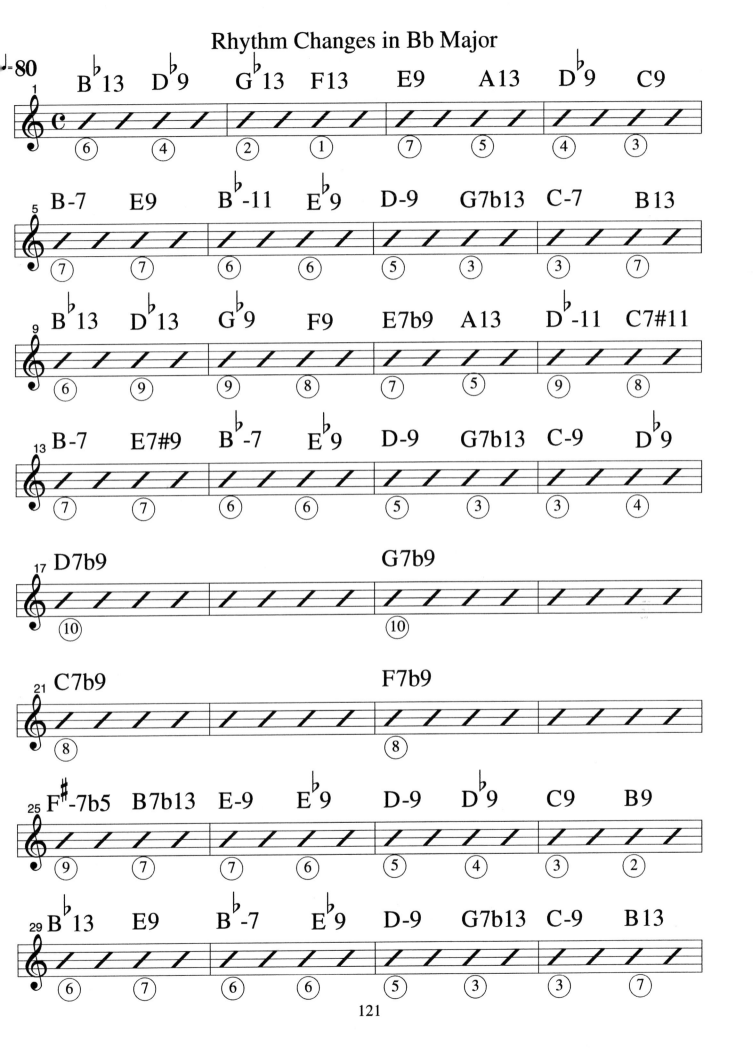

Rhythm Changes in Ab Major

Rhythm Changes in Db Major

Rhythm Changes in E Major

Rhythm Changes in D Major

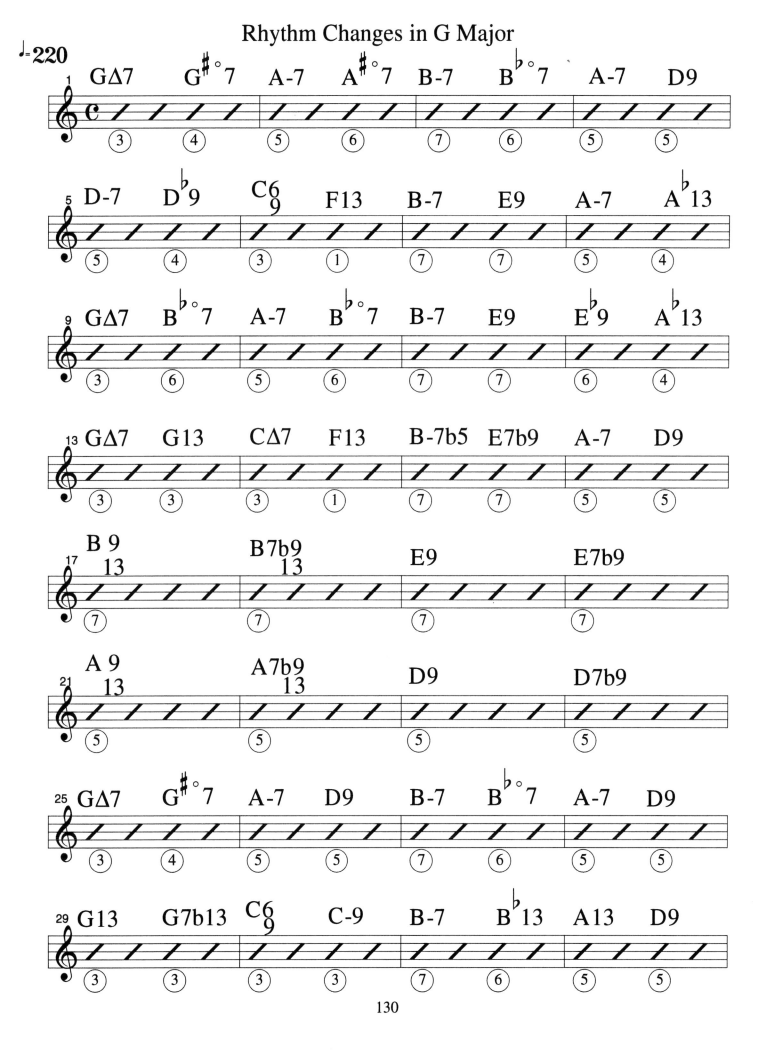

12 Bar Blues in C Major
notes only

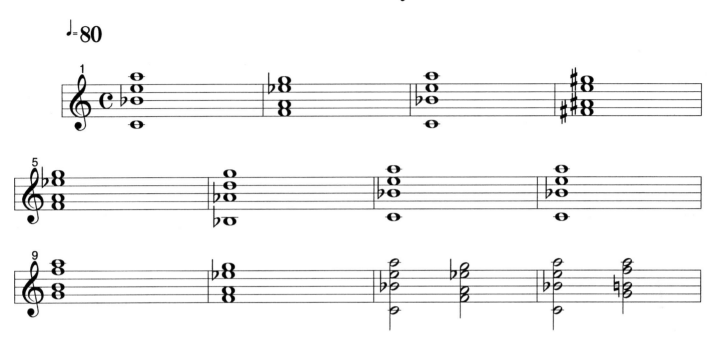

12 Bar Blues in F major
notes only

12 Bar Blues in Bb Major
notes only

12 Bar Blues in Eb Major
notes only

12 Bar Blues in Ab Major
notes only

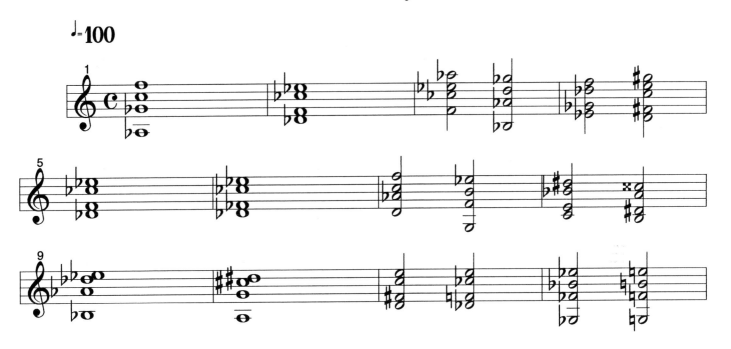

12 Bar Blues in Db Major
notes only

12 Bar Blues in Gb Major
notes only

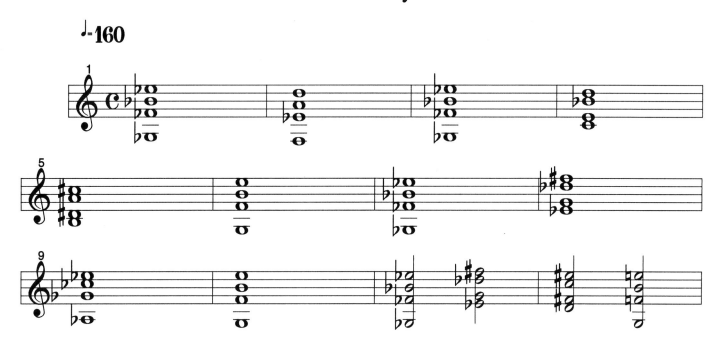

12 Bar Blues in B major
notes only

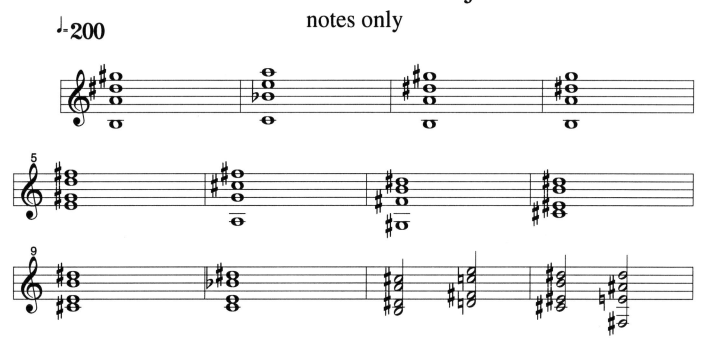

12 Bar Blues in E Major
notes only

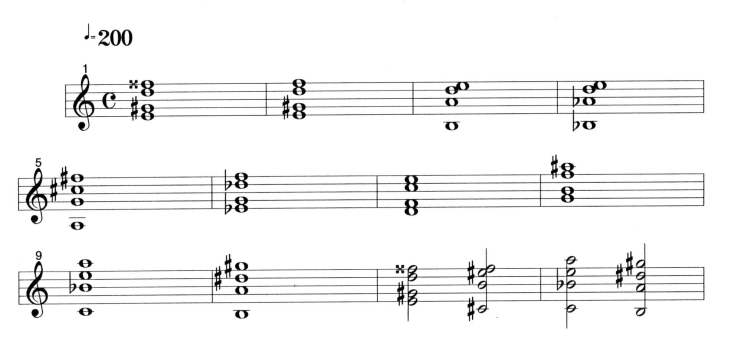

12 Bar Blues in A Major
notes only

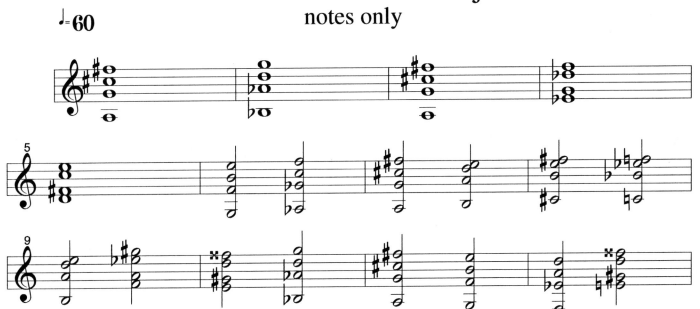

12 Bar Blues in D Major
notes only

♩=60

12 Bar Blues in G Major
notes only

♩=60

C Minor Blues
notes only

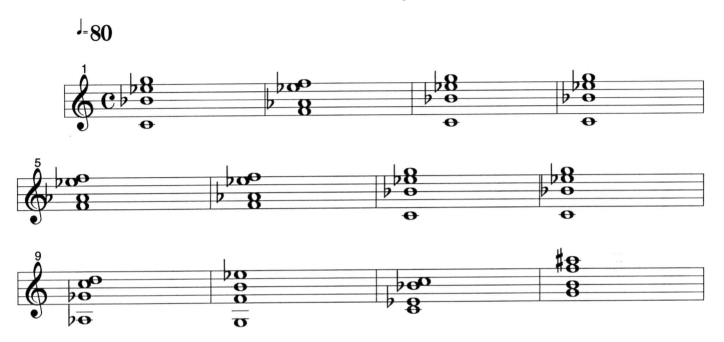

F Minor Blues
notes only

Bb Minor Blues
notes only

♩=120

Eb Minor Blues
notes only

♩=100

Ab Minor Blues
notes only

Db Minor Blues
notes only

Gb Minor Blues
notes only

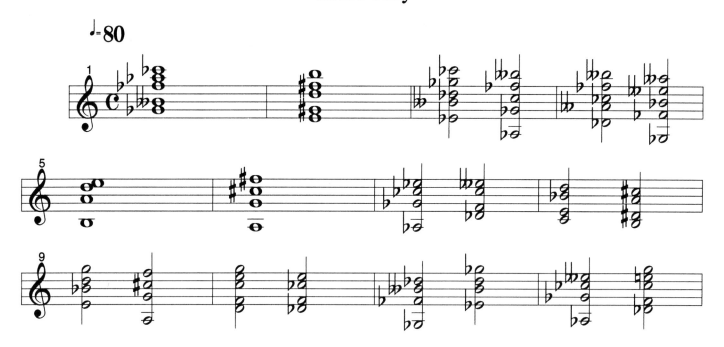

B Minor Blues
notes only

E Minor Blues
notes only

A Minor Blues
notes only

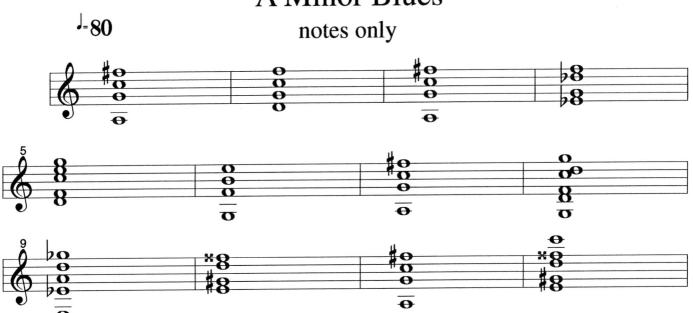

D Minor Blues
notes only

♩=100

G Minor Blues
notes only

♩=60

Rhythm Changes in C Major
with notes

Rhythm Changes in F Major
with notes

Rhythm Changes in Bb Major
with notes

♩=80

Rhythm Changes in Eb Major
with notes

Rhythm Changes in Ab Major
with notes

Rhythm Changes in Db Major
with notes

♩=50

Rhythm Changes in Gb Major
with notes

Rhythm Changes in B Major
with notes

♩=120

Rhythm Changes in E Major
with notes

$\quad \ \! = 80$

Rhythm Changes in A Major
with notes

Rhythm Changes in D Major
with notes

Rhythm Changes in G Major
with notes

Index

156

Books Available From
Muse Eek Publishing Company

The Bruce Arnold series of instruction books for guitar are the result of 20 years of teaching. Mr. Arnold, who teaches at New York University and Princeton University has listened to the questions and problems of his students, and written forty books addressing the needs of the beginning to advanced student. Written in a direct, friendly and practical manner, each book is structured in such as way as to enable a student to understand, retain and apply musical information. In short, these books teach.

1st Steps for a Beginning Guitarist
Spiral Bound ISBN 1890944-90-4   Perfect Bound ISBN 1890944-93-9

"1st Steps for a Beginning Guitarist" is a comprehensive method for guitar students who have no prior musical training. Whether you are playing acoustic, electric or twelve-string guitar, this book will give you the information you need, and trouble shoot the various pitfalls that can hinder the self-taught musician. Includes pictures, videos and audio in the form of midifiles and mp3's.

Chord Workbook for Guitar Volume 1 (2nd edition)
Spiral Bound ISBN 0-9648632-1-9   Perfect Bound ISBN 1890944-50-5

A consistent seller, this book addresses the needs of the beginning through intermediate student. The beginning student will learn chords on the guitar, and a section is also included to help learn the basics of music theory. Progressions are provided to help the student apply these chords to common sequences. The more advanced student will find the reharmonization section to be an invaluable resource of harmonic choices. Information is given through musical notation as well as tablature.

Chord Workbook for Guitar Volume 2 (2nd edition)
Spiral Bound ISBN 0-9648632-3-5   Perfect Bound ISBN 1890944-51-3

This book is the Rosetta Stone of pop/jazz chords, and is geared to the intermediate to advanced student. These are the chords that any serious student bent on a musical career must know. Unlike other books which simply give examples of isolated chords, this unique book provides a comprehensive series of progressions and chord combinations which are immediately applicable to both composition and performance.

Music Theory Workbook for Guitar Series

The world's most popular instrument, the guitar, is not taught in our public schools. In addition, it is one of the hardest on which to learn the basics of music. As a result, it is frequently difficult for the serious guitarist to get a firm foundation in theory.

Theory Workbook for Guitar Volume 1
Spiral Bound ISBN 0-9648632-4-3   Perfect Bound ISBN 1890944-52-1

This book provides real hands-on application of intervals and chords. A theory section written in concise and easy to understand language prepares the student for all exercises. Worksheets are given that quiz a student about intervals and chord construction using staff notation and guitar tablature. Answers are supplied in the back of the book enabling a student to work without a teacher.

Theory Workbook for Guitar Volume 2
Spiral Bound ISBN 0-9648632-5-1   Perfect Bound ISBN 1890944-53-X

This book provides real hands-on application for 22 different scale types. A theory section written in concise and easy to understand language prepares the student for all exercises. Worksheets are given that quiz a student about scale construction using staff notation and guitar tablature. Answers are supplied in the back of the book enabling a student to work without a teacher. Audio files are also available on the muse-eek.com website to facilitate practice and improvisation with all the scales presented.

Rhythm Book Series

These books are a breakthrough in music instruction, using the internet as a teaching tool! Audio files of all the exercises are easily downloaded from the internet.

Rhythm Primer
Spiral Bound ISBN 0-890944-03-3   Perfect Bound ISBN 1890944-59-9

This 61 page book concentrates on all basic rhythms using four rhythmic levels. All examples use one pitch, allowing the student to focus completely on time and rhythm. All exercises can be downloaded from the internet to facilitate learning. See http://www.muse-eek.com for details

Rhythms Volume 1
Spiral Bound ISBN 0-9648632-7-8   Perfect Bound ISBN 1890944-55-6

This 120 page book concentrates on eighth note rhythms and is a thesaurus of rhythmic patterns. All examples use one pitch, allowing the student to focus completely on time and rhythm. All exercises can be downloaded from the internet to facilitate learning. See http://www.muse-eek.com for details.

Rhythms Volume 2
Spiral Bound ISBN 0-9648632-8-6   Perfect Bound ISBN 1890944-56-4

This volume concentrates on sixteenth note rhythms, and is a 108 page thesaurus of rhythmic patterns. All examples use one pitch, allowing the student to focus completely on time and rhythm. All exercises can be downloaded from the internet to facilitate learning. See http://www.muse-eek.com for details.

Rhythms Volume 3
Spiral Bound ISBN 0-890944-04-1   Perfect Bound ISBN 1890944-57-2

This volume concentrates on thirty second note rhythms, and is a 102 page thesaurus of rhythmic patterns. All examples use one pitch, allowing the student to focus completely on time and rhythm. All exercises can be downloaded from the internet to facilitate learning. See http://www.muse-eek.com for details.

Odd Meters Volume 1
Spiral Bound ISBN 0-9648632-9-4   Perfect Bound ISBN 1890944-58-0

This book applies both eighth and sixteenth note rhythms to odd meter combinations. All examples use one pitch, allowing the student to focus completely on time and rhythm. Exercises can be downloaded from the internet to facilitate learning. This 100 page book is an essential sight reading tool.
See http://www.muse-eek.com for details.

Contemporary Rhythms Volume 1
Spiral Bound ISBN 1-890944-27-0   Perfect Bound ISBN 1890944-84-X

This volume concentrates on eight note rhythms and is a thesaurus of rhythmic patterns. Each exercise uses one pitch which allows the student to focus completely on time and rhythm. Exercises use modern innovations common to twentieth century notation, thereby familiarizing the student with the most sophisticated systems likely to be encountered in the course of a musical career. All exercises can be downloaded from the internet to facilitate learning. See http://www.muse-eek.com for details.

Contemporary Rhythms Volume 2
Spiral Bound ISBN 1-890944-28-9   Perfect Bound ISBN 1890944-85-8

This volume concentrates on sixteenth note rhythms and is a thesaurus of rhythmic patterns. Each exercise uses one pitch which allows the student to focus completely on time and rhythm. Exercise use modern innovations common to twentieth century notation, thereby familiarizing the student with the most sophisticated systems likely to be encountered in the course of a musical career. All exercises can be downloaded from the internet to facilitate learning. See http://www.muse-eek.com for details.

Independence Volume 1
Spiral Bound ISBN 1-890944-00-9   Perfect Bound ISBN 1890944-83-1

This 51 page book is designed for pianists, stick and touchstyle guitarists, percussionists and anyone who wishes to develop the rhythmic independence of their hands. This volume concentrates on quarter, eighth and sixteenth note rhythms and is a thesaurus of rhythmic patterns. The exercises in this book gradually incorporate more and more complex rhythmic patterns making it an excellent tool for both the beginning and the advanced student.

Other Guitar Study Aids

Right Hand Technique for Guitar Volume 1
Spiral Bound ISBN 0-9648632-6-X   Perfect Bound ISBN 1890944-54-8

Here's a breakthrough in music instruction, using the internet as a teaching tool! This book gives a concise method for developing right hand technique on the guitar, one of the most overlooked and under-addressed aspects of learning the instrument. The simplest, most basic movements are used to build fatigue-free technique. Exercises can be downloaded from the internet to facilitate learning. See http://www.muse-eek.com for details.

Single String Studies Volume One
Spiral Bound ISBN 1-890944-01-7   Perfect Bound ISBN 1890944-62-9

This book is an excellent learning tool for both the beginner who has no experience reading music on the guitar, and the advanced student looking to improve their ledger line reading and general knowledge of each string of the guitar. Each exercise concentrates the students attention on one string at a time. This allows a familiarity to form between the written pitch and where it can be found on the guitar along with improving one's "feel" for jumping linearly across the fretboard. Exercises can be downloaded from the internet to facilitate learning. See http://www.muse-eek.com for details.

Single String Studies Volume Two
Spiral Bound ISBN 1-890944-05-X   Perfect Bound ISBN 1890944-64-5

This book is a continuation of Volume One, but using non-diatonic notes. Volume Two helps the intermediate and advanced student improve their ledger line reading and general knowledge of each string of the guitar. Each exercise concentrates the students attention on one string at a time. This allows a familiarity to form between the written pitch and where it can be found on the guitar along with improving one's "feel" for jumping linearly across the fretboard. Exercises can be downloaded from the internet to facilitate learning. See http://www.muse-eek.com for details.

Single String Studies Volume One (Bass Clef)
Spiral Bound ISBN 1-890944-02-5   Perfect Bound ISBN 1890944-63-7

This book is an excellent learning tool for both the beginner who has no experience reading music on the bass guitar, and the advanced student looking to improve their ledger line reading and general knowledge of each string of the bass. Each exercise concentrates a students attention of one string at a time. This allows a familiarity to form between the written pitch and where it can be found on the bass along with improving one's "feel" for jumping linearly across the fretboard. Exercises can be downloaded from the internet to facilitate learning. See http://www.muse-eek.com for details.

Single String Studies Volume Two (Bass Clef)
Spiral Bound ISBN 1-890944-06-8   Perfect Bound ISBN 1890944-65-3

This book is a continuation of Volume One, but using non-diatonic notes. Volume Two helps the intermediate and advanced student improve their ledger line reading and general knowledge of each string of the bass. Each exercise concentrates the students attention on one string at a time. This allows a familiarity to form between the written pitch and where it can be found on the bass along with improving one's "feel" for jumping linearly across the fretboard. Exercises can be downloaded from the internet to facilitate learning. See http://www.muse-eek.com for details.

Guitar Clinic
Spiral Bound ISBN 1-890944-45-9   Perfect Bound ISBN 1890944-86-6

Guitar Clinic" contains techniques and exercises Mr. Arnold uses in the clinics and workshops he teaches around the U.S.. Much of the material in this book is culled from Mr. Arnold's educational series, over thirty books in all. The student wishing to expand on his or her studies will find suggestions within the text as to which of Mr. Arnold's books will best serve their specific needs. Topics covered include: how to read music, sight reading, reading rhythms, music theory, chord and scale construction, modal sequencing, approach notes, reharmonization, bass and chord comping, and hexatonic scales.

Sight Singing and Ear Training Series

The world is full of ear training and sight reading books, so why do we need more?
This sight singing and ear training series uses a different method of teaching relative pitch sight singing and ear training. The success of this method has been remark-able. Along with a new method of ear training these books also use CDs and the internet as a teaching tool! Audio files of all the exercises are easily downloaded from the internet at www.muse-eek.com By combining interactive audio files with a new approach to ear training a student's progress is limited only by their willingness to practice!

A Fanatic's Guide to Ear Training and Sight Singing
Spiral Bound ISBN 1-890944-19-X   Perfect Bound ISBN 1890944-75-0

This book and CD present a method for developing good pitch recognition through sight singing. This method differs from the myriad of other sight singing books in that it develops the ability to identify and name all twelve pitches within a key cen-ter. Through this method a student gains the ability to identify sound based on it's relationship to a key and not the relationship of one note to another (i.e. interval training as commonly taught in many texts). All note groupings from one to six notes are presented giving the student a thesaurus of basic note combinations which develops sight singing and note recognition to a level unattainable before this Guide's existence.

Key Note Recognition
Spiral Bound ISBN 1-890944-30-3   Perfect Bound ISBN 1890944-77-7

This book and CD present a method for developing the ability to recognize the function of any note against a key. This method is a must for anyone who wishes to sound one note on an instrument or voice and instantly know what key a song is in. Through this method a student gains the ability to identify a sound based on its relationship to a key and not the relationship of one note to another (i.e. interval training as commonly taught in many texts). Key Center Recognition is a definite requirement before proceeding to two note ear training.

LINES Volume One: Sight Reading and Sight Singing Exercises
Spiral Bound ISBN 1-890944-09-2   Perfect Bound ISBN 1890944-76-9

This book can be used for many applications. It is an excellent source for easy half note melodies that a beginner can use to learn how to read music or for sight singing slightly chromatic lines. An intermediate or advanced student will find exercises for multi-voice reading. These exercises can also be used for multi-voice ear training. The book has the added benefit in that all exercises can be heard by downloading the audio files for each example. See http://www.muse-eek.com for details.

Ear Training ONE NOTE: Beginning Level
Spiral Bound ISBN 1-890944-12-2   Perfect Bound ISBN 1890944-66-1

This Book and Audio CD presents a new and exciting method for developing relative pitch ear training. It has been used with great success and is now finally available on CD. There are three levels available depending on the student's ability. This begin-ning level is recommended for students who have little or no music training.

Ear Training ONE NOTE: Intermediate Level
Spiral Bound ISBN 1-890944-13-0   Perfect Bound ISBN 1890944-67-X

This Audio CD and booklet presents a new and exciting method of developing relative pitch ear training. It has been used with great success and is now finally available on CD. This intermediate level is recommended for students who have had some music training but still find their skills need more development.

Ear Training ONE NOTE: Advanced Level
Spiral Bound ISBN 1-890944-14-9   Perfect Bound ISBN 1890944-68-8

This Audio CD and booklet presents a new and exciting method of developing relative pitch ear training. It has been used with great success and is now finally available on CD. There are three levels available depending on the student's ability. This advanced level is recommended for students who have worked with the intermediate level and now wish to perfect their skills.

Ear Training TWO NOTE: Beginning Level Volume One
Spiral Bound ISBN 1-890944-31-9   Perfect Bound ISBN 1890944-69-6

This Book and Audio CD continues the method of developing relative pitch ear training as set forth in the "Ear Training, One Note" series. There are six volumes in the beginning level series. Through practice, the student eventually gains the ability to recognize the key and the names of any two notes played simultaneously. Volume One concentrates on 5ths. Prerequisite: a strong grasp of the One Note method.

Ear Training TWO NOTE: Beginning LevelVolume Two
Spiral Bound ISBN 1-890944-32-7   Perfect Bound ISBN 1890944-70-X

This Book and Audio CD continues the method of developing relative pitch ear training as set forth in the "Ear Training, One Note" series. There are six volumes in the beginning level series. Through practice, the student eventually gains the ability to recognize the key and the names of any two notes played simultaneously. Volume Two concentrates on 3rds. Prerequisite: a strong grasp of the One Note method.

Ear Training TWO NOTE: Beginning Level Volume Three
Spiral Bound ISBN 1-890944-33-5   Perfect Bound ISBN 1890944-71-8

This Book and Audio CD continues the method of developing relative pitch ear training as set forth in the "Ear Training, One Note" series. There are six volumes in the beginning level series. Through practice, the student eventually gains the ability to recognize the key and the names of any two notes played simultaneously. Volume Three concentrates on 6ths. Prerequisite: a strong grasp of the One Note method.

Ear Training TWO NOTE: Beginning Level Volume Four
Spiral Bound ISBN 1-890944-34-3   Perfect Bound ISBN 1890944-72-6

This Book and Audio CD continues the method of developing relative pitch ear training as set forth in the "Ear Training, One Note" series. There are six volumes in the beginning level series. Through practice, the student eventually gains the ability to recognize the key and the names of any two notes played simultaneously. Volume Four concentrates on 4ths. Prerequisite: a strong grasp of the One Note method.

Ear Training TWO NOTE: Beginning Level Volume Five
Spiral Bound ISBN 1-890944-35-1   Perfect Bound ISBN 1890944-73-4

This Book and Audio CD continues the method of developing relative pitch ear training as set forth in the "Ear Training, One Note" series. There are six volumes in the beginning level series. Through practice, the student eventually gains the ability to recognize the key and the names of any two notes played simultaneously. Volume Five concentrates on 2nds. Prerequisite: a strong grasp of the One Note method.

Ear Training TWO NOTE: Beginning Level Volume Six
Spiral Bound ISBN 1-890944-36-X   Perfect Bound ISBN 1890944-74-2

This Book and Audio CD continues the method of developing relative pitch ear training as set forth in the "Ear Training, One Note" series. There are six volumes in the beginning level series. Through practice, the student eventually gains the ability to recognize the key and the names of any two notes played simultaneously. Volume Six concentrates on 7ths. Prerequisite: a strong grasp of the One Note method.

Comping Styles Series

This series is built on the progressions found in Chord Workbook Volume One. Each book covers a specific style of music and presents exercises to help a guitarist, bassist or drummer master that style. Audio CDs are also available so a student can play along with each example and really get "into the groove."

Comping Styles for the Guitar Volume Two FUNK
Spiral Bound ISBN 1-890944-07-6   Perfect Bound ISBN 1890944-60-2

This volume teaches a student how to play guitar or piano in a funk style. 36 Progressions are presented: 12 keys of a Major and Minor Blues plus 12 keys of Rhythm Changes A different groove is presented for each exercise giving the student a wide range of funk rhythms to master.   An Audio CD is also included so a student can play along with each example and really get "into the groove." The audio CD contains "trio" versions of each exercise with Guitar, Bass and Drums.

Comping Styles for the Bass Volume Two FUNK
Spiral Bound ISBN 1-890944-08-4   Perfect Bound ISBN 1890944-61-0

This volume teaches a student how to play bass in a funk style. 36 Progressions are presented: 12 keys of a Major and Minor Blues plus 12 keys of Rhythm Changes A different groove is presented for each exercise giving the student a wide range of funk rhythms to master.   An Audio CD is also included so a student can play along with each example and really get "into the groove." The audio CD contains "trio" versions of each exercise with Guitar, Bass and Drums.

Bass Lines: Learning and Understanding the Jazz-Blues Bass Line
Spiral Bound ISBN 1-890944-94-7   Perfect Bound ISBN 1890944-95-5

This book covers the basics of bass line construction. A theoretical guide to building bass lines is presented along with 36 chord progressions utilizing the twelve keys of a Major and Minor Blues, plus twelve keys of Rhythm Changes. A reharmonization section is also provided which demonstrates how to reharmonize a chord progression on the spot.

Time Series

The Doing Time series presents a method for contacting, developing and relying on your internal time sense: This series is an excellent source for any musician who is serious about developing strong internal sense of time. This is particularly useful in any kind of music where the rhythms and time signatures may be very complex or free, and there is no conductor.

THE BIG METRONOME
Spiral Bound ISBN 1-890944-37-8   Perfect Bound ISBN 1890944-82-3

The Big Metronome is designed to help you develop a better internal sense of time. This is accomplished by requiring you to "feel time" rather than having you rely on the steady click of a metronome. The idea is to slowly wean yourself away from an external device and rely on your internal/natural sense of time. The exercises presented work in conjunction with the three CDs that accompany this book. CD 1 presents the first 13 settings from a traditional metronome 40-66; the second CD contains metronome markings 69-116, and the third CD contains metronome markings 120-208. The first CD gives you a 2 bar count off and a click every measure, the second CD gives you a 2 bar count off and a click every 2 measures, the 3rd CD gives you a 2 bar count off and a click every 4 measures. By presenting all common metronome markings a student can use these 3 CDs as a replacement for a traditional metronome.

Doing Time with the Blues Volume One:
Spiral Bound ISBN 1-890944-17-3   Perfect Bound ISBN 1890944-78-5

The book and CD presents a method for gaining an internal sense of time thereby eliminating dependence on a metronome. The book presents the basic concept for developing good time and also includes exercises that can be practiced with the CD. The CD provides eight 8 minute tracks at different tempos in which the time is delineated every 2 bars, and with an extra hit every 12 bars to outline the blues form. The student may then use the exercises presented in the book to gain control of their execution or improvise to gain control of their ideas using this bare minimum of time delineation.

Doing Time with the Blues Volume Two:
Spiral Bound ISBN 1-890944-18-1   Perfect Bound ISBN 1890944-79-3

This is the 2nd volume of a four volume series which presents a method for developing a musician's internal sense of time, thereby eliminating dependence on a metronome. This 2nd volume presents different exercises which further the development of this time sense. This 2nd volume begins to test even a professional level player's ability. The CD provides eight 8 minute tracks at different tempos in which the time is delineated every 4 bars with an extra hit every 12 bars to outline the blues form.   New exercises are also included that can be practiced with the CD. This series is an excellent source for any musician who is serious about developing an internal sense of time.

Doing Time with 32 bars Volume One:
Spiral Bound ISBN 1-890944-22-X   Perfect Bound ISBN Spiral Bound ISBN
1890944-80-7

The book and CD presents a method for gaining an internal sense of time
thereby eliminating dependence on a metronome. The book presents the basic
concept for developing good time and also includes exercises that can be
practiced with the CD. The CD provides eight 8 minute tracks at different
tempos in which the time is delineated every 2 bars, with an extra hit every 32
to outline the 32 bar form. The student may then use the exercises presented
in the book to gain control of their execution or improvise to gain control of
their ideas using this bare minimum of time delineation.

Doing Time with 32 bars Volume Two:
Spiral Bound ISBN 1-890944-23-8   Perfect Bound ISBN Spiral Bound ISBN
1890944-81-5

This is the 2nd volume of a four volume series which presents a method for
developing a musician's internal sense of time, thereby eliminating dependence
on a metronome.. This 2nd volume presents different exercises which further
the development of this time sense. This 2nd volume begins to test even a
professional level player's ability. The CD provides eight 8 minute tracks at
different tempos in which the time is delineated every 4 bars with an extra hit
every 32 bars to outline the 32 bar form.   New exercises are also included
that can be practiced with the CD. This series is an excellent source for any
musician who is serious about developing an internal sense of time.

Other Workbooks

**Music Theory Workbook for All Instruments, Volume 1: Interval
and Chord Construction**
Spiral Bound ISBN 1890944-92-0   Perfect Bound ISBN 1890944-46-7

This book provides real hands-on application of intervals and chords. A theory
section written in concise and easy to understand language prepares the
student for all exercises. Worksheets are given that quiz a student about
intervals and chord construction using staff notation. Answers are supplied in
the back of the book enabling a student to work without a teacher.

E-Books

The Bruce Arnold series of instructional E-books is for the student who wishes to target specific areas of study that are of particular interest. Many of these books are excerpted from other larger texts. The excerpted source is listed for each book. These books are available on-line at www.muse-eek.com as well as at many e-tailers throughout the internet. These books can also be purchased in the traditional book binding format. (See the ISBN number for proper format)

Chord Velocity: Volume One, Learning to switch between chords quickly
E-book ISBN 1-890944-88-2   Traditional Book Binding ISBN 1-890944-97-1

The first hurdle a beginning guitarist encounters is difficulty in switching between chords quickly enough to make a chord progression sound like music. This book provides exercises that help a student gradually increase the speed with which they change chords. Special free audio files are also available on the muse-eek.com website to make practice more productive and fun. With a few weeks, remarkable improvement by can be achieved using this method. This book is excerpted from "1st Steps for a Beginning Guitarist Volume One."

Guitar Technique: Volume One, Learning the basics to fast, clean, accurate and fluid performance skills.
E-book ISBN 1-890944-91-2   Traditional Book Binding ISBN 1-890944-99-8

This book is for both the beginning guitarist or the more experienced guitarist who wishes to improve their technique. All aspects of the physical act of playing the guitar are covered, from how to hold a guitar to the specific way each hand is involved in the playing process. Pictures and videos are provided to help clarify each technique. These pictures and videos are either contained in the book or can be downloaded at www.muse-eek.com This book is excerpted from "1st Steps for a Beginning Guitarist Volume One."

Accompaniment: Volume One, Learning to Play Bass and Chords Simultaneously
E-book ISBN 1-890944-87-4   Traditional Book Binding ISBN 1-890944-96-3

The techniques found within this book are an excellent resource for creating and understanding how to play bass and chords simultaneously in a jazz or blues style. Special attention is paid to understanding how this technique is created, thereby enabling the student to recreate this style with other pieces of music. This book is excerpted from the book "Guitar Clinic."

Beginning Rhythm Studies: Volume One, Learning the basics of reading rhythm and playing in time.
E-book ISBN 1-890944-89-0   Traditional Book Binding 1-890944-98-X

This book covers the basics for anyone wishing to understand or improve their rhythmic abilities. Simple language is used to show the student how to read and play rhythm. Exercises are presented which can accelerate the learning process. Audio examples in the form of midifiles are available on the muse-eek.com website to facilitate learning the correct rhythm in time. This book is excerpted from the book "Rhythm Primer."